D1549574

PATRON SAINT
OF EYELINER

CREDITS

PATRON SAINT OF EYELINER
Jeremy Reed
A Creation Books Original
ISBN 1 84068 042 3
Published 2000AD
Copyright © Jeremy Reed 1999
All world rights reserved
Photograph of Jeremy Reed by John Robinson

AUTHOR'S ACKNOWLEDGEMENTS

This book was made possible by a supporting cast of angels: Lene Rasmussen, John Robinson, Annie Maclean, Owen Michael Brown, Stephen Andrews and Stephen Barber. The author would like to thank everyone at Creation Books, and particularly James Williamson for enthusiastic support and encouragement.

For Fanchon Fröhlich

"Genet's writing is about dying, about anticipating death, about dedications to the dead, about feeling already dead, and he is complaining even at this point, 'Life is what's missing'."
—Edmund White

"Concentrating on their [the Beach Boys] widely recognized obsession – technological advance – they took off for Holland where the surf's never up and went through some half a million dollars settling in and arranging for nearly four tons of flying studio, a prototype for the future, to be brought from America. The evidence of the whole incredible adventure is on their new album..."
—From a Warner Bros. press kit, Nov 1972

"And if I die before I wake up
I pray the Lord don't smudge my make-up.
The dress will be fine when the hem I take up,
The dress will fit just fine."
—Marc Almond, "Saint Judy"

PATRON SAINT OF EYELINER

JEREMY REED

GLAMOUR, LOVE AND DEATH

Kate Moss

Disingenuously quotidian,
she's like the smalltown girl in a pop song
we think we know but never meet,

an off-the-shoulder pigtailed archetype,
a romanced in the rainy park ideal
who surfs it on to glossies –

a knee-boot ritzy catwalk mode
of being in the close-up image pool,
designer complemented, runway-chic.

She's boy-shaped, tubular, with fizzy style,
an Englished, latter day Alice
retrieving money from her shoes –

Court style purple hocked in the gooseberry bush.
Her metaphor for love's a rainy day
the drops all heart-shaped, glittery

glissando bringing comfort in its hits
across a bubbly taxi's bump
to red-alert. Mad citified crisis.

Kate's shoot should be an ostrich ride,
hair dressed in feathers, and a cherry bunch
mobbed at her lips. Black clouds in a white sky.

She's naive, Essex, but alive
to beauty, and the unzipped moment's sharp
distillation of lime not shock lemon.

Quentin Crisp As Prime Minister

Recalled at last for a pink happening,
the sassy Whitehall ceremonials
proclaim his mordant camp sagacity,
his drag investiture, all brimmish hat –
a UFO concept in mauve felt,
his costume jewellery's glitz vocabulary

pronouncing all values are paste,
but better known for the truth in the lie.
He's come by water, for the river speaks
consolably to the outlawed,
and queened above its moody soup
on purple cushions, he's forgiven all
who spat upon him as a travesty
of mismatched sexes, hunted him through streets
and builder's yards down to the river's crawl.

From barge to a pink-frosted limousine,
he's had the car stand under foggy trees
in St. James Park, and kept it back
until irreverence returned
to his coquettish dignity.
He dispenses red roses to the crowd,
bitches with performing artistes

who mob his progress, and all over town
the streets are scented with Chanel,
the army disbanded and cloned in drag.
They're waiting for his inaugural speech,

an end to biz-speak rhetoric
and ministerial duplicity.
His timing's perfect, and his drawl appropriate
to London's liberation, and he points
to absence of the police, and higher up
to roses trailing smoochily
round Downing Street's redoubtably barred gates.

Yesterday When I Was Young

In memory of Dusty Springfield

Mimosas, Dear, forcing lemony scent
into a cold, reactionary March wind,
I bought them on the day you died
to raise a yellow torch in memory
of how your voice addressed our needs
in every shade of love that's blue
and shared with us its aching entreaty
to find a little sunshine after rain,
a sanctuary from bruises dealt
invisibly across the soul.
Today, your death-day, you are on the air
posthumously, your husky R & B
slow-burners building in their rise and fall
smokily pitched delivery.
Your life returns with every anguished catch
in phrasing, you the bouffant blonde,
the patron saint of mascara

wreathed in a boa, lending signature
to how the song hinged on a frantic sob
to make the pain definitive...
I keep on hearing retros of your voice
as though you're still singing familiar hits
six hours after your death. Big purple clouds
arrive, dispensing hints of flashy showers.
You've gone away, like someone takes the train,
with no-one knowing, no address,
no destination, no reporting back
about pure music on the other side.
We listen to you in Freedom, First Out,
and hold you near this way and celebrate
a torchy diva's dramas, feel the hurt
in your vocal authority,
and hope you're healed in passing, wish you where
the light in its entirety shines through.

Elvis Presley At 40

The walls are black fake suede in buttoned strips,
a bedroom like a car's interior
sealed off as though the King's already dead,
his body grown to be an elephant's,
a creature out of climate in the South.
He sits in state on a red coverlet,
nursing an automatic, levels it,
and blasts a wall-pinned photograph
between the eyes. He'd reinvent himself,
retrieve the snake-hipped Lizard King
if he could find a way to kick
the drugs that snow into his brain.
He's draped the mirrors so his eyes won't meet
the facially rotund, 20 stone hulk
inhabiting his room. Gold pyjamas,
hair blacker than a funeral car.
A rhinestoned, Las Vegas gladiator,
he lives inside that time-warp, clings to fame
like someone holding with both hands
to the roof of a speeding train.
He's lonely in decline. Each new decade
invalidates his image. When he eats,
he puts a coating on despair,
a cheeseburger cushion over the drop.
He spades into his sixth banana-split,
then fires a second shot to have an aide
come running to his room. It's always night
inside and out for him, a night
that leads to his dead mother, and she waits
to guide him through a long tunnel
into the greater light. He waves to her,
and she salutes him with a torch.
He's happy now. The gold discs on his wall
are blazing planets, and his forty years
slow for a moment like an animal
dropped to the dust to lick its hurt,
or Gladys all those years ago
holding back tears, sending him off on tour,
crying through laughter on the Graceland porch.

The Rolling Stones

Sainted by notoreity
they're photographed by a bulldozered site,
cables exposed to bypass-overhaul,

the hotel backgrounded as a glass cliff.
They're King crows parading in leopardskin
and cavalierly biffed knee-boots.

They wear their legend in deep-grooved skin tracks,
as though a creature roughed a hide
in crocodilean epidermis.

It's like they've died and been reborn again,
played tricks with time to always be the same
persons trapped by a hedonistic warp.

They're liver-indestructible,
four decades of rocky empties glitter
behind them as a slaughtered galaxy.

They've burnt up continents in a cortege
of funeral limos. Thunder in the air.
The town silent, like it awaited sacrifice.

Guitar power's only half of it:
the singer's rush drives a trajectory
that hangs the moment between blues and death,

the skimming bird dipping the waterfall
shattering white force in a pool.
They've written rock riffs into history

and never stood back from those energies.
They're scorched by chords: their artistry's
enduring as pharonic dynasties.

They stand exposed to hard Miami light,
dark glasses keeping the intruder out
and wait to gun high voltage at the night.

Beddoes

Suicided clean out of British poetry,
remembered like a chemist mannequin –

prop-head for dark glasses, Guerlain stockist,
'Jicky' as a window display,
and something like Bavarian cow parsley

bleeding a scent for elegy,
and a boot making its own tracks down the street

rubies lighting the severed stump
like a bracelet frozen round a wrist.

Joy

Exuberant geni
bottled by Patou
no floral interloper
challenges its high.
Its optimal note-range
is almost falsetto,
but contained by a hauteur
imperious as Callas.
A nose in 1930
had the geni swim
in the amber cocktail's
vivacious alchemy,
staged it for backless
or low-cleavage dare
a mood permutator
crowding on the pulse,
the flower-code cracked
to feed the geni hits
for its habit.
Grasse Jasmine solos
top of the scale,
Bulgarian roses up there
as supporting No 2,
the rest are a fusion
of targeted scents,
surprisingly pertinent
when teasing the nape.
The geni's a stayer
without dramatic come down
leaves like a sunset's
effusive glower,
offers hints he'll linger
until dutifully resummoned,
atomized on call
for a stage-struck renewal.

Naomi Campbell

She's sleekly pantherish, the leggy strut
in vaudevillean ensemble – Westwood plumes
or an azalea pink Versace sheath

updates the beautiful, her miffish lead
dispelled by feline poise, she's up on points
a resonating chord, a double-bass

dictated by her hips. She wins the shoot,
queen-cat electing through a second skin
to give designer striptease dignity,

buttocks triangularised by a thong...
Her life's redeemed by moments out of time,
her upturned green crocodile handbag spills

a Hermes diary, teased Marlboro Lights,
a Louis Vuitton wallet, favourite things
like Jolly Ranchers sweets, a Guerlain scent,

the clutter of a personal repertoire.
Her lip-scar blemish is the little flaw
she notes as reassuring – it's her own

comforting imperfection left untouched
and proudly vulnerable. She gives new line
to archetypal glamour, and re-zipped

catwalks thigh-split audacities, salutes
the impish moment, rides the crest like surf
sounding the world's beaches as fanned applause.

Patron Saint Of Eyeliner

Palace Gate

In memory of Martyn Sinnott

The Bentley wasn't yours; you nicked a wing
zigzagging on the flyover, burnt West
from the main concourse, 'look no hands' –
your risky up-there dynamic when coked
imparting crazy flash to how you drove

to win the precedent at every light.
Your clubby years, no focused energies,
sensation always pitched to overkill,
then lost again, you ran up every stair
to punch the rainbow in the chandelier

and come down disillusioned by the dawn.
You torched your youth and never wanted more
than to derealise before the crash...
I see you dragged-up in outrageous mink,
bitchily witty with camp repartee,

disarming friends, but always in reserve
compassionate, as though a kindness won
the deep place in your heart. Our zippy days
return now shocking-pink azaleas
overcrowd with their hectic ballroom gowns

in every London park, dramatic reds
ready to sashay the season's catwalk,
then tumble, turned over by raunchy winds.
Sometimes I lift the telephone to hear
it ringing in your old palatial flat,

as though by a freaky coincidence
you'll intercept the call, and say 'I'm back,
death offered no more fulfilment than life.'
Your jumbled, heirloomed rooms at Palace Gate
spread out their contents in my memory

as though I'm back there, you so shot with AIDS,

the virus worked you cell by losing cell,
its undercover clever breaking down
your every resistance, but dignity;
you lying wrecked on a pill-hailstormed bed.

We'll never know each other twice the same.
I work in time, with all the business
you envied once, and you are open space
as I conceive it, someone, everyone,
a reincarnation with a new name?

Our big nocturnal happenings, the trust
we placed in love and death: now you've known both
and ripped the red curtain protecting youth
from rapid exposure, and hurried through,
impatient, you said, to begin again.

Drug cocktails extended your legacy.
You lived for whiskey and sweet memories,
before they too were wiped. I buy you flowers,
today, to keep you near: a heady shock
of rain-scented, abundantly clear-eyed

and piercing jonquils, and see you again,
this time in full health running for the car
with expectation life lay round the bend,
the clear road open wide beneath the stars
and in its curved reach pointing without end.

Buying CDs

The everydayness of the kitschy act,
her blue mascara's inked a track
from smudgy Soho rain, so left-profile
she's mourning Elvis, a tadpole

suspended from an eyelinered cat's eye.
She's going sixties – icon stuff
rectangularized – "Aftermath"
shrinkwrapped to fit a pocket, Jagger's mean
demeanour fronting a decade

in hipsters, polka-dots,
his lips exceeding limits like a rose.
He sights her in his random dealing-cards
flurry of racks, snapping at names

like somebody running down stairs,
and he's attracted to the way
she's introspective, dreamily
pooling in blue eyes, backstroking that blue
to climb into a little boat.
She swims surfaces of the sea within

to meet the dead, Billy Fury,
Roy Orbison. So on. So on.
He can't get her into his sight,
she's more taken up with eponymous

heroes on mid-price: Scott Walker.
She makes a purchase, goes back out
to muzzy rain in shiny boots
patented like a berry's shine,
and he keeps searching, singing to himself,

'Baby come back, Baby be mine.'

Star-Struck

Mostly they whisked a Dino on the straight,
coaxed its potential to a feeding roar,
a scarlet bolt of sonic energy,

and she was leathered, with pink hair tied back,
and he was concentrated in a frame

windowed into a blue vanishing point.
That summer, fuming, meteoric skies
had stardust cooking in trajectories;

white noise was subsystemed all over town.
The two bounced signals back off each other,

remained exclusive, contained by a car,
coding its mechanistics with their own.
Rain on the road sounded like bubblewrap.

The nights were big with star-warred holographs,
or just another species programming

its molecules to fit with ours. We heard
the Dino rupture quiet, storm the dark
in a spectacular out to the coast.

Nothing was seen of theirs, but ritual.
She'd sit on the red bonnet under trees
as though meditating on ways to break

the grid, and jump reality. He'd drive
by day, and she by night. Stones blasted by

on weird configurations overhead.
The two seemed star-struck, aimed to meet the pull
of fall out blazing through dust-corridors.

Gothic Laboratory

1

The first steps underground were choked with leaves,
October's free-fall blackening.
A sequinned Rolls stood leaf-blotched in the field.

2

The blonde sat watching in a tree,
her leather jeans tight as a condom's grip;
her backbrain modemed to the galaxy.

3

Impulse-translation pickups in the door.
A man swims like a white shark on a screen.
The blonde touch-tones remote. A star comes on.

4

Three paramedics dismount from a jeep;
the blonde keeps tuning, ejects a cassette.
The men retrieve it in a haloed glow.

5

Leafy diffusion. In the underworld,
they're bioengineering pineal glands.
They'll one day get the whole consciousness frame.

6

The star comes closer. It is bluish-green.
The weird one sits inside a chill-out room
niched in the techno-harassed corridor.

7

Three horses, black coats stamped with stars,
browse into view. They're somewhere else
sniffing the future's twitchy silver trail.

8

Stardust keeps blowing through the field.
The blonde lies horizontal on the branch.
Everything fizzes with the rushing hail.

A Moment In Time

Line it, like coke cleared from a tabletop,
the head blown back, or like the scarlet rose

voluptuous, magicked before the storm
skins it of apple-scented skirts,
the flash undeviating rain

full-mouthed as a soprano.
Know it, like a face never seen again
that stays for ever, someone in the crowd

running to catch a train.
Hear it, like Billie Holiday

subjectivizing lyric; on repeat
the song is always present, grainy tone
got grave on liquor.

Touch it, like nerve-tones in a cat,
the untameable jaguar
or water chasing over pebbled frets.

But celebrate the going, mind banged up
with the intensity, as waiting clear
the pilot opens out to full throttle

still on the runway, nose lifted to go.

SAINTHOOD:
ELEGIES FOR DEREK JARMAN

Sainthood

The river swallows thunder; cold gold nerves
sheathed in its spinal undertow:
it keeps on filming clouds stoned by the light.

Someone's in trouble diagnosed
penitent HIV. Their viral load
reads like a print-out from the galaxy.

Sainthood's conferred by heavy rain,
it's like the red rose swallowed by Genet,
found in a ruined cemetery.

What's it about a man converting earth
salted by sea-winds into flower
speaks of the street-crowned apotheosis,

the jeaned Soho iconoclast
transforming everything he saw
to lyric as it opens in a flower?

Life's a reminder that we die;
the gutter takes a footprint, and returns
the indentation as pure gold.

A man cries out at Charing Cross,
his moment used up, but continuous
in what imagination colours blue.

He's here to stay: the autumn surf
gobbles a shingled gradient, ejects
slow-release burials in its shattered tow.

People Come And Go

She'll tell you in her phrasing, love and death
meet at the apple's core, the yellow skin
bruising sweet black. The words travel her breath

as torchy consonants, her sequins drip
like red flame sheathing a tropical fish.
She coathangers a right hand to her hip.

When he remembers the black diva's tone,
he dips into a wasp-filled memory.
An apple cuts its bootlace, thuds on stone.

Memory's like a clouded lily pond,
Elizabeth and John Dee look up through carp.
There's Pasolini, windowed in a bond

with broken things. The sea turns frisky jade.
He feels the T-shirt wring wet at his ribs.
The viral heatwave allows for no shade.

The dead are transparent. They're light on light,
programmed into their separate energies.
Big purple thunder clouds surf through the night.

The living never outnumber the dead.
The diva's melody springs back to mind,
it's Gloomy Sunday': he retrieves the thread,

and hears the sea leave white shoes on the beach.
He lives inside the moment: it is round,
and almost orange, and just out of reach.

Burning Brightly

Summer means poppies: splashy opiates
tangoing with a swishy breeze,

giving the big come on in fuming silks,
rubbing their dusty eyes with black,
dresses in scarlet tatters, frizzy stems

notched with green Adam's apples, or the white
and purple opium poppies sleep
in a vision of the dead

sleepwalking as a slow cortege
arms lifted heliocentrically to the sun.

Somebody waits there in the noon,
a man in contemplation of his life
as though he stood in a mausoleum
hearing his voice go pleading for

a little respite from the cold
that's underworlded in his blood.
The sea sounds like it's slaughtering a bull
across the shingle. Feedback roars

through a haze spooking the coast.
He stands in discourse with himself,
head bowed, and hectic poppies prove

consolatory, burning bright
and fragile, like a lip trembling with love.

Love In Death

All day, the traffic's ambient decibels
surf around Phoenix House, its flat facade
presenting on the street. A white-noise shell,

the building's atomized by toxic haze,
its windows click-tracked by the diesel mash
of black cabs streaming up to Centre Point...

Somebody's absent from the honeycomb,
and uncontactable. He's gone away,
leaving a trail of sand down Brewer Street,

as though he'd walked in beach-shoes to his death,
thinking the sea was on the other side,
a blue invasion at Piccadilly.

The inspirational genus locus gone
from his packed studio, we have the word
resituate his fireballed energies

in every meeting-place where we collect
to burn a torch beside the river's groove,
or wait for love to hurry through the rain...

Say that we recreate the little things
that gave an apple-polish to his life,
a coffee-tang to being just a man

alert and vulnerable to everything,
then he's still here, beating in every heart,
catching the raindrops and making them sing.

Under Paddington

Rain over Paddington, and underground
chimeras ledge on obsidian thrones.
They'll drag him into death through corridors

serviced by no communicating line.
A messenger in a red coat will lead
his impulsed holograph into the maze,

somebody newly arrived from a day
busy with doctors, and invasive drugs,
a man nerve-sheathed inside a hologram,

still formulating scenes he'll never shoot,
or paint, the reverse mirror-side of light.
He sees his guardian's feet have dark blue soles.

The Circle line is coffin-shaped. The map
he reads, as he imagined it, is blue,
the youths who give him flowers, know he's dead.

The garden's somewhere, but it's not his own,
wired up with driftwood totems, blasted by
the wave's white thunder fuzzing on the air.

He can't turn round on the committed road;
his name is typed into the microfiche.
The boys around him spray his aura gold.

London's behind him. There, it rains all day.
The river's foetus carries a new god
shock-waved along its lightning-twitchy spine.

Retrieving Angel

Whose is the hand extended in the dark?
He doesn't see the face, the concave back
shimmers with vertebral translucency.

The psychopomp's uplifted feet are bruised
with pink magnolia petals. In the park
the youths transmit after-death frequencies,

his flashback-recall is to Hampstead Heath
with outlaws grouped beneath an orgy tree,
the rainy oaks brimming with violent scent.

He's in a garden, and its mauve and blue,
the urns are packed with rubies, glowering jewels.
He has to check himself for deja vu.

The one in front has shoulder-length blond hair
and answers an awareness that's so fast
that thinking has become pure energy.

Two red-haired angels dressed in leather jeans,
are watching new souls on a terminal.
The dazed arrivals twitch at memory,

then quickly relocate to being there.
He presses on; the light is clearer now.
The angel looks round: he is in his teens.

They keep on moving. It's like going home
to meet himself again in the deep end
of a wild garden's blue completed shade.

Sites

A warehouse burns in solid orange flame,
erupts at Bankside, a black cumulus
of tented smoke pyramiding the Thames.

He sits and contemplates biography,
a Persian carpet rages in the sky,
voluted purples peacocked into green,

a fuming skylight over Canon Street.
A city's dawn is always visionary,
he strokes atomized stardust on his skin,

as though chasing gold embers from his pores.
His studio is torched. The years go by
memoried under bridges, blued with tears,

the same trains hustling into Charing Cross,
the changes registered inside his blood.
A day is like a pick-up which won't stay

faithful to anyone, despite the need
to have it open out into a friend.
Bugloss and borage present to his eyes...

He paces memory like it's a room
in which the furniture comes clear at dawn,
a blue vase loaded with redundant dreams,

a red one choked with flowers, he clears the lot
to know the moment, catch his breath again,
and feel the city fit him like a boot.

Obsequies

Sit in a gold sequinned gown on the shore,
a man blasted by toxic chemicals,
increasing, as his T-cell count
zeroes like stars receding in deep space.

Is it the sea's stony dialectic
at Dungeness, invites his charged
inventiveness to know itself
bright as the dazzle blow-waved off the beach?

Or listen along the South Bank side,
where time sits on the river's back,
a young man in a floppy beret drops
a white lily into the tide

as a small death in memory,
washed away in the cloud-piled afternoon,
like youth gone downstream to return
decades later as someone else

burnt at the edges from a different shore.
Yellow horned poppy tugs its roots,
resilient like scabious.
The hand that planted is clawed by a drip.

An anchor's ochre rust erodes
a staying power that won't go,
an object obsoleted by the sea.
With man it's different: he can't get back

to know himself again, not twice the same.
This one's ending is Derek's, cell by cell,
as though the sea forced inland, wiped the lot,
but left a camera aimed into the clouds.

GOING VIRTUAL

Road To The Stars

Mindbender's virtual pad's East Hollywood;
the mink-trimmed black silk roses shocked
beside a window-clear green negligee

busted by a bra-popping Jayne Mansfield.
He lives V.R. most of the day,
freeze-frames obsessions, like the stunt man's run
burning a 50s Porsche as Jimmy Dean
along Ventura Boulevard

and out to 46, hair blown away;
the supernova impact imminent.
Mindbender works a studio
with ambient permutations, meets no-one

except on touch down from his groove.
His neural highways overload
with digital biographies.
The cat's drunk on chopped kangaroo.

His girlfriend's violet suede thigh-boots
are watermarked around her crotch.
She doesn't know much of reality

and prods it like a mismanaged chopstick
feeling for some particular.
Her headphones live on her like space stations
feeding her loops from Jupiter.

Mindbender makes adjustments to real time,
dead-ends his fantasies, jumps in the car
a Deanish, open Porsche affair,
his girlfriend curled into a leopardskin,
and zips attackingly out to the coast
in search of mutants where they infiltrate
amongst off duty pilots talking skies

around a silver holographic bar.

Poetic Objectives

A Cadillac burns up the dust-road West,
a burnished, chrome artefact, somebody's
idea of a recording space.
Most vision travels West. The shape of time

is still apparent, past and future meet
as interacting tachyons,
a backward travelling William Blake's
the cyberpunk inside the Cadillac
pushing a road towards the sea,

the many waiting, thousands dressed in black,
for the collective word's morphology
to be delivered. The Pacific pours
effluvial blue diamonds at their feet,

a dead whale's headed round the coast.
A life-affirmative posse, a troop
expecting the miraculous, they count
the real turn-ons as shooting stars,

the brightest angels on a maxi-screen.
Back of the car, he dreams of a gateway,
an orientation to the seamless join
in which vision becomes reality,

and they are dancing on the beach
for messengers, for contact with the way
a poem steps out of the sun,
today, tomorrow written in its core,

the planets silent for the space of half an hour,
somebody standing in the visual frame
stars on a profile by the open door.

Poetry (In The Making)

You skin the onion, while I camp the line
with glitter metaphor, impacted zing.
You always cook in a black negligee

to learn the sensual harmony of things
adopting each other inside a sauce,
a sort of herbal frisson alchemy.

I keep my insighting irreverent,
catwalk the pieces from the underworld
into an O.T.T. apprehension

of image striptease. Alcohol's a part
of firing up the system, hitting speed
into freaky neuron activity.

Your hair bubblewraps into marabou.
The cooking takes on lifted earthy notes
and settles in its hints as salutary.

I work a medium called glam poetry
and try to give a dazzle to the thrust
of verticalising the ordinary.

The poem's news inside the global house,
it's this year's model, shaped that way by words.
I like mine in stilettos and black seams.

I grow distracted, like I'm on a flight
that should be landing soon, I'm not sure where,
except the terminals are blazing now.

Coffin For A Cutie

Somebody's story. It begins that way,
the word concurrent with Big Bang, the voice
permutating to pulp fiction,
a Spike Morelli book 1950,
the cover showing Cutie, stockinged legs
provocatively arched on a coffin,

her red sashaying gown a stereotype
moulded to the curve-conscious vamp.
You think she'll use the coffin as a bed
to satisfy her necrophilia,

or end up inside, buried in that dress,
a victim of the murderous cocktail:
sex, two-timing and twisted jealousy.
The dictates of her possible story
involve A's resolution on the stairs.
B's inside feeding on her abandon,
they're head and tail of a consuming snake

which wants to eat itself.
B sucks a gold tooth, and cradles his gun.
The word originally lit the stars,
orgasmic supernovae patterning
brilliant galactic vertebrae,

light as transmission through the universe.
B picks up Cutie's cuban heeled nylons,
his Colt .45 having done the trick.
They're tinted with her Chanel. Now he fires

a controlled beam from a tachyon gun,
and Cutie's resurrected, still in red.
Another story. And the two embrace
over the dead man lying on the bed.

Lucinda

He cooked the car: a Porsche skinned of its gloss,
an impact-artefact left by the road,
some sort of commerce with apocalypse

having him free-associate for days
middled in wasteland on the Isle of Dogs,
a toxin readout fingerprinting haze.

She placed dark glasses on his consciousness
and fed him comfort in her penthouse tank.
A red sun windowed itself like a fish.

A blonde Lucinda, spraycanned into jeans,
she coaxed him info of her software cult,
the ones who shot movies in people's heads

and convened once a month in hyperspace.
He relocated real time, but stayed on,
and changed the colour of his eyes, his name.

She zapped his past in a re-earthing rite.
Once, looking out, he saw his wife and child
searching the road; the underground carpark.

He'd been recoded; they were aliens now,
another species sniffing for his facts.
He stood in vinyl, arms raised to the sun.

Autumn brought fog: he knew his own by then.
He scanned the screen for imminence; she sat
waiting for lost ones in tight leopardskin.

Beauty And The Beast

What I'd imagined, crenellated towers
gobbled by lozenged ivy, fuming mists
dry-iced over a sunken lake,
a black swan-shaped boat tied at the jetty,
the weirdo sitting on a ledge
cradling a bottle of his blood

blueprinted with dysfunctional genes,
an eye watching from every leaf
in the occult ecosystem,

was a coded metaphor on the road
of daily experience, how the blonde
walks off the beach into a wood,
and doesn't know why she's compelled to force
a blue door sunk into a wall

bushy with blackberries, and once inside
recalls she's still wearing a bikini
and nothing else, she's come too far

autonomously. And he knows it all,
the segregated weirdo living out
his traumatized disfigurement, his car
climbing one wet day off the bend
to crash inside a meteoric sun.

She's fascinated and decides to stay
until rhinoplastic innovations
help restructure his face. He thinks he's dead
despite the loss of damages,

and she intended to leave anyway.

No Future For You

Crosstalk from other planets, and the ranch
conceals an underworld bunker
wallpapered near-space cobalt, empty blue.
They've let the horses break across country,
a red-gold stallion, Rising Sun,

gone like a streaming fireball on the wind.
They listen out for planetary music,
a global mix, digital notation
that has the silence sing, the tumbleweed

and morning glory collect sound.
The two wear uniforms, Army fatigues.
They are their own appointed paramilitary,
splashy with badges and the hero cult

abstrusely centred on the nameless one.
Visitors talk of dead malls, franchises,
the Presidential car found abandoned,
the radio tuned to 1978,
freakishly intersecting with the past

still going on immediate,
the Neo-Nazi music breaking bones,
a hummingbird sipping a flower nearby:
amalgamated sounds invade the noon,

Balinese genggong, Amazonian chants,
brainfever birds, beluga and bat sounds,
and sometimes a primitive drum.
They listen on the porch. Indolent heat
raking up horse-smells, and the President
arriving in a bloodstained suit,
hands in his pockets, nothing on his feet.

Novels

Obituarized data on the microfiche,
they stay suspended like ice-burials,
cryogenic bodies in nitrogen

awaiting recall. Reconfigured lives.
Most are sucked into a black hole,
imploded star that won't give pieces back
or redress the issue posthumously.

I see cerise camellias flattened out
by April rain, when buying books;
the light's translucently reverential,

a wine-blushed afterglow on Holland Park.
Anna Kavan at Hillsleigh Street
writing her fiction, needling smack,
heroin for talcum powder,
dead on the bathroom floor, a borderline

absolutist cult
bringing her weirdo wacky novels back.
I stand outside the garden where she sat,
a bottle blond with crushed lipstick,
seeing a leopard under trees

seeing her absent body break in flames.
Survival's hers. Another rain
of books arrive, the story lasts
for ever in its modulated ways,

new lives, new fiction in the DNA,
and each attempt a shot to have it end
to write the whole thing down.
Kavan in Chanel. Elegant, cut-off,

stylized, obsessive. Faxing from the dead?
I keep her in mind as a holograph,
leopards and hypodermics on the bed.

Leader Of The Pack

I saw your blue coat on somebody else,
a memory corona, tugging thing
like listening to the Shangri-Las,
their broody atmospherics,   Leader Of The Pack',
in which the biker joins the early dead,
the leather cortege in the cemetery,
a devil-angel logoed on each back.

I miss you more than I can ever say,
and synchronistically, coincidentally,
that girlie group's vocalised elegy
turns up on the airwaves, all thunderstorm
and moody trauma with her heart broken
beside an oil pool on the road,
the sixties still beginning, and that song
hanging on it like a blue rain,
melodramatics teased by the big sound.

October, and a fuming pinkish sky
is slashed by late afternoon mauves.
We've lost our walks through Air Street, Golden Square,
the buzzy Soho afternoon, the shift
into those small streets with their quiet,
the headiness of things we said. I keep
most days inside, go out about the hour
darkness drops over town, and hear the roar

of leather bikers burning up the air.

Pandora's Box

A smoky corridor; the twisted stairs
are like metallic vertebrae
dead-dropping to a basement.
Initials chipped as scratch-vocabularies
are signs of those who came and went,

deliberated on the box
and wouldn't dare flip back the lid.
Airbrushed in bold pimento red
I read the name, James Dean, and higher up

Triple X, Jackie Kennedy.
So many made the pilgrimage,
left cars waiting outside, debated all,

and walked back to the road, disconsolate.
Firearms are mounted in the hall
of this hermetically sealed house.
Two jackals guard the steps,

gold collars, gold studs underfoot.
The box is like a jewel casket
secured by two mirror hands. Current jabs

an aura round the artefact,
a premonition of electric shock;
potential to autocombust
with the speed of a photographer's flash,

should the wrong hand risk everything.
We have to die to know Pandora's metaphor,
but for a moment think we'll blow the lot,

and stand there shaking under a spotlight
pooling a white eye on the basement floor.

Glory Road

All wired-up visionaries pursue that road,
a red sun in the smashed ozone window
fumingly declarative – West go West –

explore the ruins, they'll return again,
Arthur Rimbaud, Jim Morrison,
as permutations in the gene,
invaders on another beach,

icons infiltrating the Internet.
And will they ever know the light they've been?
receive the flashback inside a bookstore

scatting their own books as somebody else?
Look to the morning glory as it snakes
a blue roof through the stringy vine,
a way up high, less desperate,

than shooting lyric through the heart.
And if one came back, would a sun-baked barn
remind him of delirium, the fight

to write a poem on a whiptailed snake.
The right road's the one to the stars,
seen through an arch beside the shore,
with surfers frisking rides in white moonlight,

appearing as the new species
delivered by the waves' stupendous roar.

Crusoe

The surf was a subliminal soundtrack,
a tape-loop fed through inner dialogue,
and if a storm bashed up the seamless blue
of sea and sky he searched the beach
for soggy traffic, squeezed sun-lotion tubes,
an orange ball, a plastic shoe,
and best of all a pin-up magazine
flapped in one squally day, its splay-legged nudes

affording him an erogenous map;
he dried each page, and licked the snaky curves.
Quillai and eucalyptus, mango, coconut,
he got to know the rich vocàbulary
of trees, and watched the liners pass
outside his reality-grid
and guessed his life ran parallel

to theirs and every other dimension.
At night his undulating fist
burnt an invisible tattoo
over his solar need. He worked at it,

creating a simulacrum,
and sculpted models from the sand,
sand-women, upright, prostrate, on all fours,

a diagrammatic harem.
Mosquitoes left hot bites along his skin,
a dead whale rotted on the shore.

And when he heard two girls laughing, he knew
they must have put in from a near island.
He watched them in their tanga bikinis
a million miles from him, stretch out on towels,

within easy reach of a white canoe.

A Writer's Day

Tea like a smoky bonfire on the tongue
co-ordinating with the nerves, a jab
and then another jab. I pick out lines
from the subliminal blue room,
sampling images from the ambient
reverberation a poem transmits;
the music I play imitates
the process, patching on to dub bass lines.
A spiky London day, the hyper hours,
a quizzing telephone, I teleport
the friends I need into the flat,
cancel appointments, find two dead light bulbs,
wonder what year it is, console myself
whatever the month, autumn will come soon
like a mad woman dressed in red
doing a striptease in the street.
Letters arrive, a stray squirrel looks in,
the hours take on the trance autonomy
created by weird narrative;
I make big lateral shifts across the page.
I'm headed somewhere, and it's almost dark,
alcohol as a stimulus, and out
to meet somebody after a long arm
crispy and hot-paced lick around the park.

Cyberia

Victor adjusts his goggles, and the street
is a distorted, wide-angle blue haze,
blazingly splashy, a phased software Las Vegas,
a limo lasering to the sidewalk
showered with sequins, and it's always night
inside his metaverse, a geometry
of neoned artefacts. He likes to sit
in his Frank Lloyd Wright house that's up on screen

and rest from brainfade, VR overdose.
When he re-earths, he's been that far away
he's lost to where his hands and feet
are creatures of support. Another street,
called Whitfield Street, is there outside,
white sunlight slanting through the Soho afternoon,
and suddenly rain-jewellery
flashing across the stunted scene,
a squally, uptight April day. Blue day.

Victor is split along a dimension.
Mostly it's sleep he fears, the imageries
different again, autonomous
mauve turtles crawling through the underworld,
a system built into the brain.
Reality is the metaverse.
He space-glows for ten minutes, rights his eyes,
goes out and mounts his silver bike,
aims for the asteroid-belt, roars away,
his helmet studded by the liberal rain.

London By Day

All in their milieux, written underground
along the tube-map's arteries,
she with her Janet Reger carrier
under Vauxhall, fastforwarded across
the villages, and I am ending up
compact Soho, Livonia Street

in jazzy intermittent autumn rain.
Once, in the Tottenham Court Road underpass
a denimed junky spooked me, no body,
just the projection of himself.
I find apocalyptic signs down there,

numerals, disjunctive lexicons.
The Northern Line is sketched in black, the red
is Central. Blake gets out at Bank,
the angel with him wears a gold catsuit.
A rainbow points up over Waterloo

the tail-end lit with poetry.
Hurry, I tell myself in Poland Street,
there's things you haven't done, a way with words
is no credential in this crowd.
Endgaming cuts out the immediate.

Wait on the corner for a special sign,
like sunlight lasering the sopping leaves
in Soho Square. Half London's going down
to snatch a tunnelled journey, and a lion
waits with its keeper at the subway gate.

Data Angels

A back alley wall studded with fake jewels;
the pilot left his flying jacket and blackbox
on the window-sill. The girl leaning out
has information in her eyes,
data spaced in two hazel terminals.

I enter cyberspace like that;
angels have come alive, they're everywhere
like consciousness, as though seeing has points
and radials the way stars shine

more brightly, the blacker the night.
I think I met the pilot in a field
a year ago, he'd crashed the plane
and couldn't find it on the mountainside.
He played his blackbox tape on a Sony Walkman.

I stay parallel to myself
on information highways. It's the multiverse
I've entered, I can't touch or reach
the android in the thigh-high boots
picking a heart-shaped pink cloud off a shelf.

Patron Saint Of Eyeliner

Angels

"Every angel's terrible."
—Rilke

What if they're all around me in the light
owning to parallel topographies;
print a negative in reverse
the skin areas turn black, a white
defining edge gives the face boundaries.
I never see myself asleep,
the action in the dream is narrative,
I make it happen, hidden out of sight,
a blue eye blinks on every forest leaf,
we wait on a wooden bench for a train
which never comes, you wear black espadrilles
and hold a finger to your mouth.
I'm given back these small particulars
inside a still interior light
with you ten thousand miles away.
If I believe in angels, it's like that,
and when they meet us, they're autonomous,
fluent as photons. Outside, there's an owl,
silent, immediate to its prey,
eyes bigger than red suns to their vision.
What if I need help, will a telephone
big as a tree fall in my hand,
the right number stored in its memory,
fall like lightning at my feet?
Angels are in the human too,
the Monroe legend, a slinky white dress,
an early death, somebody in this street
who knows me from a different life,
swinging a head round over a shoulder
as if affirming that it's really true.

Frequency

Thunder is part of this, and overload
straining the circuit, as I listen out
for lyric directives, the voice
laying a line down – is the first take right?
for writing's like a frequency
connecting nerve by nerve, a chancy jab
at what's around. At twelve I flicked
a switch and heard Leonard Cohen

involuntarily, immediately,
the voice sounding out of a deep
hiding place, and a desert poured
glitter over each syllable.
The accident was like catching a star

I'd never let blow out. Today, I crossed
Waterloo Bridge, and got the connection,
a poem as it travels impulses,
the river tracking down below
in bronzy greens, a white ferry
jostling with tourists sliding into view,
the sun a coronal fractal,

the word transferred to the back of my hand
before paper, and all around
the city's urgent communications
transmitted block to block, while a new contact
is made with poetry, the miracle's

brightest, clearest channel finding a beat
on that dimension, while helicopters
are overhead scouting a traffic queue,
and thunder builds behind oppressive heat.

DIVA CULTURE

Female Singers

So often reaching out of ruined love
to find a high spot in their pain
a way to sensitize a loss
that's universal in its suffering,
and up on heels, red heels spiking the boards,
she dips a hand into her heart
to feel the broken places, lets it bleed

through the phrasing, and her backless gown
is raining sequins to the floor.
Sob sisters, torchy divas in the spot,
all tousled hair and red cupid's bow lips
they're like a black sheathed sisterhood
who plead right to the roots of love
as though by never letting go
they'll win the lover back, or die from need.
  Cry Me A River' sung so deep it's down
wherever breath begins.

They heal us by companioning their hurt,
and living through it all day, every day
as truth that feeds a tear-stained voice
in telling how a woman's dream
was broken on that downmood night
he met somebody else, and went away.
It's the old story of a life
thrown out, betrayed, and after all the years
still loyal, as she thrusts a gloved hand high
and holds the note like putting in a knife.

Broken Hearts

There should be heart-shaped rooms in which we sit
as a collective to repair
the damage done by love, and half the night
we'd exchange stories, share a common pain
that's always different, but never less
in how the ruin's total, like a house
slipped off a cliff-edge to the sea
or like a turtle that has lost its shell
but keeps on going, making tracks on sand
to find a refuge up beyond the surf.
We're all suddenly disinherited
from little ways, familiar dialogue,
security of someone there to share
bad news, rejection, a red letter day,
a downmood's tumble of blue dice,
or someone there to celebrate a quiet
in which the meaning is in being two
without a need to speak. But out of love
we seem to be falling down stairs
that never terminate. He left or she
took off with someone else, it's like the blow
will never stop arriving in the heart
as an impacted fist. We'd call the place
Heartbreak Hotel, and hope to patch the scars
of unrequited love and leave
a little less in tatters, disrepair.
I'll find the place one day, and book a room
and talk amongst the losers of a face
I can't forget, and of a special hurt
bleeding like footprints scattered over snow.

Shirley Bassey

Storming my space with vocal flourishes,
she estimates how big a thing is love
in her delivery, fills out
the constant knowing of a broken heart
in histrionic phrasing, turns it round
dark mood to light then dark again,
takes up the story and the lyric sheet's

smudged with mascara from a finger dab
at some offending irritant.
What's it about her, Queen of Broken Hearts
professing loyalty despite the hurt
touches me where the break won't heal
to shut out my own recent green-eyed loss,
has me distracted all day in my flat
raising the volume on repeat
hanging my life on every sustained note,

frightened that when the music stops
the red-haired memories will overtake.
Voice as a gestural overview
on unrequited love, her feeling tone
colours the line to thunder clouds,
drops to reflection, looks for a way through

then grows resigned to irreparable pain.
Cathartic, sewn into a sequinned gown,
she throws her arms up, reaches out
for consolation in what might have been
answerable love, torches the song
to burning monuments, exits in flame
and bows as the percussion crashes down.

Femmes Fatales

His photographic mythomania
with images tacked up on every wall,
how does that lipstick ever get to glower
like a smudged autumn berry, matt or gloss
in bruised reds punishing the mouth,
scarlet satin or mulberry
pigmented to a volcano, the touch
the artist added as an afterthought

which burns as central flourish, Clara Bow
or Paloma Picasso
and every legendary femme fatale

preserving sensual mystique, all black clothes
and leopard's eyes, soprano voice
acting as counterpoint to how her legs
arrange and rearrange themselves.
Each gesture is theatricalized.

His fixation was with that look,
so many glossy black and whites
mounted and framed, archival, obsessive,
he hunted that felinity
and lived with it, right to the lipstick tubes
discarded by the stars. His walls were black,
his carpets pink, his furniture silver,

he grew apart, blacked out mirrors, and wore
the highest heels to cross his cobalt floor.

Diva Culture

The piano lid slammed down and temper out
as though a cat sprung from a lake
direct into a boat, and rocked its squat
dead-centred, balanced equilbrium.
The unpredictable. A storm
a day, tragic identity
with hurt and separation, is a man
a woman, a woman a man?
No money all week, but extravagance,

red roses crowding by the bed,
burial requests sealed in an envelope,
and then that hostile arena, the street,
unthinkable without dark shades
and impacted auric mystique,

a diva's lonely misunderstood days.
Zombie lyric sopranos, torchy queens,
concealed exhibitionists, they sound out
a need along the gender gap,
a place in which pieces don't fit

coherently, but a gloved hand
flies up, and for a moment heads spin round
amazed at the temerity
of someone wiping daylight off the map
by their dramatic statement. Do or die.

Mystique

Green houseblinds drawn all night, all day,
mystique is like a fern, so intricate
it patterns sensibility
and argues for a very private space
in which to find a resonance. What's new,
what's gone, are equalized in time
by being individual, closed doors
admitting only what is valuable
to some advancement. There are names fit that,
Proust, Garbo, Callas, Presley, and the ones
who never exceeded a cult, the ones
who stayed anonymous.
A different blue
to solitude, and a shader perverse
as abstract quality, mystique attracts
a self-destructive defiance, he got
his habit like that, she a way
with margaritas through an afternoon
that never stopped, and somehow turned rumour
into an actuality. What's there
behind the blinds? The question puts up spines

like a challenged hedgehog. Removed, far out,
and mostly ill, he got that way
the King of Rock and Roll walled in Graceland,
surrounded by gold discs, gold Cadillacs,
bloated by eating disorders, but loved
for every note delivered, and his bed
became the confines of his life,

dreaming for years he was already dead.

David Bowie, 1995

Cool in the Chateau Marmont, and the sky
is wide Pacific cerulean blues.
Day-glos arrest the nearness. Sunset Strip
hangs in its balance on the earthquake flaw,

apocalyptic reverb underground.
He's there as a millennial survivor,
a louche, quirkily English artefact,
the image altered to prevailing breeze,

the late 20th century technophile
invested with exultant bonhomie,
the youthful profile intact, eyes attuned
to widescreened bilocated frequencies.

Another Marlboro. His compulsive need.
Most art is damaged nerve. Its freaky pulse
jumps in the stratosphere. It's like a bird
crashing a windscreen but it goes on through

confusing, stabilizing to a beat
which gives it integration. Death's the trip
excites him by its possibilities,
a weird electrics infiltrating cells,

another booster disappearing act.
The Great Pretender's strained, left-handed voice
disquieting, sampled, driven to the edge,
flavours our urbanized insanity.

Black jeans, black eyeliner, he's reached a place
of looking at cut-up through a window.
Space-boy hieroglyphics. The future light
burns on his nerve-drive as live energy.

Scott Walker, 1996

No-one in the spaced-out, unurgent days,
lost to touristic anonymity
in Bayswater, dark blue glasses for eyes,

a passive-alert sensibility
still listening for the inner voice
to reconnect with breath, to bruise with song.
And all the empty days, they're like autumn,

autumn which never leaves a park.
His impetus is frozen; in a glass
he sees his solitary, constrained life

bleed to relentless subjectivity
between whisky shots. A cinema,
an off-license, an iron gate
open into the underworld,
he has his night itinerary,

invisibility.
And will it come again, apocalypse
telescoped by a voice, the tone reading
an elegy in which we're all involved
like buffalo stampeding towards a black sun?

He's waiting for the final call,
an angel to step from a car,
leave something on the road, a sign, a word,
an indication that his work is done,
five after midnight, by Holland Park wall.

Stormy Weather

Take me so bluely, greyly, stormily,
and always blackly, inconclusively,
into that bluesy, jazzy song,
it's Lena Horn, or Billie Holiday,
perhaps even Sinatra's rounding out
of love's moody, sad inequalities
I'm playing on this rainy day,

reflecting on old unrequited love
left like a red glove on the beach
for the highest wave to retrieve
and scoop into the frothy swash.
Don't easy couples marry on the beach? ⤚

a black car standing by for a white dress
a black dress standing by for a white car.
Billie could find no equal in a man.

Pre-thunder clarity, and sassy pinks
luminous under density
building as massive cumulus.
Something will break; a sonic riff

bring back the sharpest memories,
the ones that bite like lemon juice.
I play it over, "Stormy Weather",
the way she gets the rhyme on 'together',
before the vampish hurt breaks through
gritty with memories, and the fast rain
orchestrates every shade of moody blue.

Camp Innuendos

Prose panached by Anais Nin;
the pronounced gesture turning a phrase round
and out of gender. Masc as Fem.

Dramatization of the little thing;
rhinestones as a vocabulary,
a beret worn in dumpy rain,

the downturned mouth an arch
staged poppy-red.

Buying pink carnations on a Sunday,
and later divaesque torchy parentheses

that wailing voice between glossies
got for the fashion shoot

and lavender notes in a tea.
A boa round a gilt angel,
the world outside mashed into autumn leaves,

red like the sheath sewn on Rita Hayworth.

Listening To Leonard Cohen

For Annie

Blue atmospherics of the late year fog,
an insulating ruckus, I can hear
a foghorn out there in the bay,
declarative baritone getting through
a sometimes undulating wall
a blowy white shirt wider than the sky.

These days I backtrack on the songs I knew,
and reacquaint myself that way
with years gone missing like an aircraft lost
in wailing fog, and realise
how deep a state of mind they are
Cohen's simple lyric expedients –
Songs From A Room and Songs of Love and Hate
right to the quirky I'm Your Man,
and always solitude sits in a chair
back to the watcher, playing a Jew's harp,
a red rose crushed beneath each foot,
a woman's name written on the window.
The blond sun checks in later. Days go by.

His lyrics are a mood-vocabulary
searching out corners in the heart,
last desperate places where we hide from love,
a heart in which old rusty ships anchor
and decompose. I play his songs tonight
and every other night, and a full moon
is out behind the fog, and I can hear
a master bleed his pain with melody.

Shrouds

A Leonard Cohen formal concert suit,
black, single breasted, invisible stripes,
worn Montreal, 1979,

detachable gold shoulder in one arm.
Or a Greta Garbo black slip,
a Gina Lolobrigida baby-doll,

they're all mortuary possibilities.
A black feather boa tied round the waist,
Turkish pyjamas or Gestapo coat,
clingfilm sprayed with a blue sheen,

or someone sealed inside a precious stone,
ice or an amber honeycomb.

Wilde scrutinized the zinc table
inside a Paris morgue, but was denied
appropriate to him a sequinned gown

or anything with a mink trim.
Poe would have needed a skull and crossbones print,

Monroe maribou-edged satin,
and not the proletariat white sheet

hemmed from the crown to curled blue feet.

Roses

Suggest fellation from a diva's mouth,
and I am carrying this slow-burning

single rose through a London street,
compacted thunder at its core,

a glowering claret overspill of skirts,
a torchy pasha on a thorny spine

I'll place reverberating in your hands
as storm delivered from my heart

before expectant loud vitrescent rain
whips clinging ghost against your skin.

Rilke stage-managed pink roses
searching through involutions for the eye

mirrored in his pineal aperture,
the third eye, Shiva's, seeing through the stars.

Sighting his end at Charenton
De Sade ordered profuse midsummer reds,

trampled them stem by stem into the mud
razoring beauty with his split-end nerves.

My token shivers in a nervy hand,
sultry locket-shaped petals bleeding scent.

I'm effortful in getting there,
your thin-lipped downturned smile sensing I'm late,

uncertain if my flowering fist
contains a snake's head rattling for the bite.

Iced Buns

Vision communicates along the road,
fireballs like oranges at the window,
spontaneous as consciousness

grabbing instructions from their speed.
We search for jobs inside the wind,
and talk iced buns at a table,
a jagged chocolate fringe cliffhanging the edge,
hundreds and thousands roofing the sweet slick

canoed into the palate. There's no ode
to iced buns, apricot pastries,
the sticky side of poetry.

A box
is ribboned like a coffin, a mauve sash

on the sarcophagus.
Eat the vanilla ones while reading Blake.
Jerusalem built into Paddington,

hot jewels blazing at each window.
Mine's chocolate, and yours baby-pink,
and I'm planning to write vanilla odes.

Late 20th Century Fairy Story

She never compromised, and kept apart
moodily clear that she would find her man,
trigger an internal timer
to know the dagger punched through a red heart
intensity of love tinctured with hate,

the apple spiked with cinnamon.
She caught his eye inside a shopping mall,
and later outside when his convex back
was lifting a gold box into the boot,
she noted gold, despite the trade logo
stamped on cardboard, and there were jewels
spilling across the container,
she wasn't sure. The car was black

and black each time she looked again,
then gone.

If it was him, a black-quiffed Elvis type
sighting her above CD racks,
that second time, then she found in her hand
a heart-shaped ruby and it burnt.

She met him three weeks later in parkland,
he was just there beneath the trees,
and leaves were flowering from his hands and feet,
and there were cords around him, and the pain

had brought him ecstatically to his knees.

Saintmaker

Penthoused above the river, foggy days
cropped by a red upstaging sun
insulate private hours. She reads a book

on a circular mirror floor.
Putti with insolent red pouts
are collaged icons staring down,
image contemporaneity.
Her bathroom's all black marble. Monroe's head
on hot and cold gilt taps,

a serendipity's rococo kitsch.
Later, she'll light a candle, dress in white,
and draw blinds on the river view,

riffle the letters from a P.O. Box
containing photographs, shuffle the pack,
reading a Tarot in the random signs,
and try all over again to select

a lover as potential saint,
embellishes their photos with felt-tips,
the right one, wrong one, possibility?
Strips naked with surprise at one,

confers a sainthood, and arms open wide,
stands on the terrace to salute the sun.

Patron Saint Of Eyeliner

Making Holes In The Moment

A beach-tanned strawberry in a bikini
the model gets up from her towel.
It's 1963.
Tomorrow, it's two thousand and something,
the blonde-swathed Bardot is consigned
to the collective imagery

thumbprinting time, the assemblage of frames.
Acid sprayed across nylon is an art
which burns·configuration on the dot,
the artist in a protective jumpsuit.
Auto-destructive overreach
leaving no permanence,
flaming flashback,
the impulse gone for ever. Someone else,
is it Claudia Schiffer, reads her youth
in lapidary blue waters at Capri,
the clouds stuck on the surface like mountains,
a moment's immobility

before the ageing process speeds on up?
We overtake the second, near to death,
fly with a speed that won't come down,
remember perhaps at the last moment
the blonde star on the beach that summer's day
giving a buzz to every eye in town.

Mohair Jumpers

A Goth appendage, mostly pink or black,
absolute in irreverence
to fashion dictates, asking to be stroked

the right way like a longhaired cat
submissive to sensitized fingerpads,
a jumper as a mutant cat,
shaggy like other metaphors,
a raffish bird's nest, beehive bush

twiggily bare in January.
Worn as a sixties louche ethic
to provocation, the mohair species
resurfaces on latter day

nostalgists for quiffed singers, pointed shoes.
I keep mine wardrobed, give them pulse
all winter on my back, my arms,
and leave them to dream summer through,

abandoned shock-coloured apotheoses
packed in the dark. Sometimes I think I hear
a mohair liturgy to cold,
an invitation to the diamond frost
to be resolute, early in return,

a collective voice raised to the ice
and all its polished sculptures burning clear.

Bottoms

A sensual epic, they facilitate
an eye gratified by reverse features,
a nut-shaped, heart-shaped, square, horizontal

or vertical rectangle, curved the way
a pumpkin displays firm convexity
and where the cleft is a dark crescent moon
the hand fits under that divide,
exact congruity.

It's the rejected blindside, brought face-up,
compact in Swish jeans, prominent
in a polka-dot bikini,

right cheek, left cheek, gluteal vocabulary,
the complimentary half to pouting lips,
lifted by high heels, a jelly
wobbling beneath the patting spoon,
or so the walk on ball-bearings creates

in any Southern street.
Louise Brooks, Mae West, Marilyn Monroe,
we can't recall their rhomboidal buttocks
without thinking of strawberries,

a strawberry prized between finger and thumb.
The eye is hesitant finding that mark,
flickering over its morphology,
best angled, head dipped, bending down,

hips out, and spread on its dividing line.

Danger

And if the seam had split, the fabric halved
across a square bottom, the line

verticalized from a pound cake
or any cellulitic metaphor,
we would have seen Marilyn blindside nude,

her skirt left like a tulle mould,

the zip grounded lightning on the floor.

Bitter Blue

The stylised gesture – it's behind her knees
Monroe's indelible Chanel

arriving like wind tipped with strawberry.
I number her among the ones I've lost
who enter into a big room
in autumn, combining fog out of mussed hair.
One of them steps into my dream
and leaves behind a letter I can't read.

Sadness is the shape of the underground,
it's like an armchair, left out in a field
to fill with rain. I'm passing by

or passing through, they are the same.
I wonder if they'll stay with me beyond
the wishing, 3 sweet syllables, her name.

Spleen

(after Charles Baudelaire)

I'm like the obsessed king of the rain country,
rich tyrant listening to Charles Aznavour,
locked up for days and huddled on the floor,
gold horses stabled, dogs knocked out by drugs.
Nothing excites my misfired circuitry
not even shockers from my pet drag queen's
outrageous bedside story repertoire
bring me relief from my dystopia.
My bed's all black feathers and scarlet drapes
a monument by which my harem dance
in see-through panties, but I'm dead to flesh,
my sex needs angels, androids, in-betweens.
My doctor tells me death's like alchemy,
transmutation of viral blood to gold,
pure celebration in the getting free.
I'm cold like some cryogenic film star
awaiting resurrection in the ice.
My veins are fed by underworld traffic,
sluggish, cholesteroled, and I hug the night
listening to rains write my obituary.

The Romantic Agony

Death on the highest stair. Perversity.
Byron prepares to torch his sister's hair
if she won't strip for him on the Steinway,
her bottom tattooed from a bite
he'd used to halve an apple.
His silk turban's spiked with a ruby pin.
His wife's upstairs pairing larkspur

with royal blue delphiniums.
Baudelaire dyes his hair green, shocks the crowd,
spits at himself in the mirror
premonitory to sitting half the night
pretending that he's writing, and the page
is scored, inexplicably full by dawn.

Endgamed into an alley
the last offenders disappear
as though the film continues somewhere else,
keyboarded score, scenario
unfolding on a windswept beach.
Byron's two hundred. Annabella lines

cocaine on a black fishnet knee.
Swinburne retrieves his whip, goes down again
punished by parallel red lines.
Death on the highest stair, and thunder clouds
move on the city, roof a stadium

in which the singer slaps the microphone,
sends reverb surfing through the crowd and crawls
right to the edge, and in an instant's gone.

GLITTER

Snail Tracks

A Tate and Lyle zigzag-slither,
a viscous glitter like a river broke

along its frozen spine, smashed vertebrae
blocked into iridescent shiverings,

the big undercover flaw still to rip.
A snail's filigree cryptograms

are self-created moonlight – spotlit tracks
as though this spongy lunar craft

instructed a dark star with dazzle.
A mollusc that's chewing-gum grey,

its antennae quiz the microwave
for bounce-in extraterrestrial frequencies,

signs of a blueprint somewhere else,
a boulder-sized red Martian snail

humping across the Crater Pyramid.
What is a snail mapping on the back step

with such deliberation in the shine
afterglowed by a jumpy rain

crowned into ricochet-detonations?
The snail leaves paste-lightning, a toothpaste smear

on surfaces worked over with a touch
gumming vocabularies to grit.

I stand and watch a website open up
around this journeyer, and catch myself

lifting my feet to see if stars
brim as a residue of standing still.

Hip Hop

Elative, celebratory, high again
as though a Veuve Clicquot lit through my blood
at 9 a.m. a vivifying tang

tonic as vetiver, green seas in rain,
of course a new book by John Ashbery
blows all my fuses, space to read
across his meditative latitudes,
New York a surreal artefact
hallucinated in a Cornell box.

These days the parapsychological
places a VR lighthouse in the room
and on an Ashbery day, outside as well.

What am I doing spiked in bed
on metaphor as uppers? It's the rain
enhances discourse with poetry,
the rain's like a love letter to the solitary,

an undermusic sort of elegy.
And Can You Hear, Bird is a hip hop map,
a Tarot shuffled accidentally
to throw out allegories in the fog,
the hanged man frying sausages
inevitably upside down,
the method's in free association,
and outlaws gather on the edge of town.

Friday Afternoons

Black, double-breasted, cashmere coat
got from a market. I sight you in that
headed for a connecting point –

the tube's narrowing arteries.
40,000 million gluteal cells
giving your bottom Mae West shape,
and all those flash-by stations, black-out stops
to Leicester Square.

Fridays have space, an opening up
of routinal constrictions. There's more air,
a peony-coloured underside to clouds,

a driving impulse to be free,
a bonfirish scent peppering.

Friday's a two-way mirror to infinity
viewed as a linear corridor.
I know you're headed Little Newport Street

in black court shoes.
I buy a pineapple. A lost Friday

amongst so many, it was like today,
De Sade finished a book at the Bastille,

telescoped the rolled parchment in a hole
and watched the stone around it bleed.

Henry James' Chequebook

It would have got you anywhere.
He never doodled figurative stuff,
reflex pin-headed drawings on his stubs
or ever free-associated life.
He never had a leopard print cover
or zany snakeskin, never crazily
wrote out a cheque for three million

and placed a gun beside his bed.
Money meant formal affluence,
no lack or need, a circumspect cash-flow.
Not like a poet's impecunity,
the walls written on for paper
and later written on in blood.

And all those novels big as continents
laid marble floors on the psyche.
What if a madman ran through screaming up
revenge on rationale, his mismatched shoes
loud as one purple, one orange

whizzing in livid clashes through the hall.
James never wrote poetry on his cheques
or asked for them on personalized
red and blue papers, stars and stripes detail.
He never met a Breton or Hockney.

His cheques were interesting for precision.
The poet lacking busfare, sits it out,
blows on his fingers in the cold,
waits for the fire to blaze through, grabs its tail.

Dark Matter

These windfalls, bricky Coxes left to bruise
in orchard grass, turn ciderish,
boozy with ferment, they fit blue shadows

to exact size all afternoon.
Often they cloud across my consciousness,
moody eclipses, not total,
and always unpredictably

morphing a private underworld,
the king trying to polish black shoes gold,
a serotoninised alchemy.

Black matter lies beyond the Milky Way,
explosive potential, and black holes too,
a handful of their compressed dust

weighs more than Earth.
I like to think of light reaching my hand
after 100 million years travel.
Stardust chases inside my chemistry,
molecularized from supernovae.

It's day and night and night and day again,
cannibal black holes cruise the universe.
I raid my inside contents, feel the pull
that brings me down, the out of sorts

unspecifiable blues, which will turn
to brightness later, savouring a red apple.

Yellow Roses

Three need a neck-brace after rain
discrowned a perfect sit,

all that completion, simple as Chanel,
now spilling into satin overlap,
cliffhanger narratives around for weeks,

the fallout slow-motioned, then absolute.
These yellow ones are chinnish completists –

they'll go it to the end. They're like ourselves,
broken, but unwilling to break,
the flaw inside the wineglass unobserved

until it cuts the lip.
Love is a doll with sewn-up eyes,

the stitches only taken out in dream.
We no longer see the damage that we do

to each other, messing that way
with control-panels on sanity.
Kamikaze hysterics leaking flame.

Often I cut roses when they're over,
afford them shelter and a private death,

tumbling subsidals in a waterglass,
hairdos undone from chignoned crowns
and pick up petals as they fall

like the cold silks of a deserted bride.

Out-takes

I

A Cadillac rusts in the arroyo,
they're shooting film down there, she starts to run
towards a mirror. A jackal stares back.

II

The helicopter over Centrepoint
distributes animated holograms
the size of sequins. She picks up a bear.

III

The time warp quivers imperceptibly
across the fast lane, when she floors it through
her skin turns silver in another century.

IV

The singer behind magenta ray-bans
is seeing things on acid. A black ball
runs down the white mane of Niagara Falls.

V

He's keying in postmodernist haikus
while she positions a dissolvable tattoo,
a red serpent by the iliac bone.

VI

Late afternoon on the desert island,
the ecosystem choked by blue algae,
they try to make love with no-gravity.

Jeremy Reed

VII

His database includes an astronaut
who dematerialised got back to Earth,
but still lives as a vibrational frequency.

VIII

He drives across the border, software shares.
A television's on beside the road.
The hitchhiker has narrow silver eyes.

Novel In Ten Chapters

Ch 1

I sit holding her red shoe in my lap.
Paris in late June burns in the toe point.

Ch 2

I've grown so much older since the last line;
the red shoe castanets it down the boulevard.

Ch 3

A desert island. The helicopter's
confronted by a pink bird twice its size.

Ch 4

The tree bears nothing but one violet fruit
packed with galactic hallucinogens.

Ch 5

I write I miss her. She's in inner space
a marvellous continent on which neuron?

Ch 6

Room service by telepathy. The sea
has nine tenths covered this floating hotel.

Ch 7

Sunflowers, chrysanthemums. They smell of rain.
The sun comes indoors, when I think her name.

Ch 8

The chambermaid is Elvis Presley's niece.
She hums under her breath, Heartbreak Hotel.

Ch 9

When we go under in the deep blue sea
I'll have the brightest fish carry her shoe.

Ch 10

Death is no coda. In the coral glow
I'll count the spines on a sea urchin's shell.

Petunias

Floppily laid back as loud primaries,
their catwalk attention's horizontal,
no leggy vertical axis
having the eye beanstalk its way
to richer promise – a heart-shaped bottom,

a thong presenting the divide.
They make their statements low in summer frocks
or splashy stripes, matelot tops
candied with blue or red on white,
lipstick their way to attention.

Other entropic activities flame –
nasturtiums furnace like cool meteors,
geraniums transmit an oily scent.
Petunias simmer. My right knee's an Alp
butt-faced over their lazy daze

their two after noon siesta.
If flowers ate ice-cream poutily
lipping their stamens on a spoon
then these would go for Haagen Dazs
pistachio or strawberry.

They're motion-sensors to my mood
its up or down irregularity,
the static fuzzing in my cells.
This one's shocking pink overspill
places a girl's name in my empty mouth,

shape-lifting syllables.
Nose to them I'm arched like a cat.
Purple's my favourite overture
to meditating with them, this purple
dense like a love bite placed below the waist.

January

All month I smell canned air of long-haul flights,
hear engines modulated in the sky,
Boeing traffic, air-wave reverb,

as though you're leaving all over again,
as though I haven't known you gone for good
these past five years, the vertigo
flashing into my abdomen
at news of every jet.

I used to hope a bird would bring a rose
from you, a jay stop off
in the garden, unload its beak,

a head-crested, shrill avian
scattering blue tits into sketchy flight,
a white winter rose with the scent of you
left on the cracked stone steps, and as a sign

a trembling blue feather.
January's lyricized by owls,
and New York, where you are, is under snow,
the Hudson windowed with blue ice.
Twenty below zero.

I look towards the crocus's mauve tip,
communications with you in my heart,
the always marvellously impossible
reunion on a Paris bridge,

one clear day at the year's explosive start.

Late Flutter

Nothing a knife clean through the heart
or sticked cherry wouldn't metaphor.
December has fisty camellias
pink on the undersides disturb
the notion of pure elegy,

cold writing in a robin's heart,
love as it bruises on the telephone,
impacted reproach in the ear's helix
catching me unawares like storm.

I nudge a bottle to defence,
a red unsteady pour. A second one.
So much Bordeaux clearing my cells,
autumnal sunlight in a glass
red as a dense attack of massing woods.
Your accusations clean me out,

I'm stripped to jammed confusions in my nerves,
a signal overload.
No least appeal like reaching for your hand
to channel fingertipped tactility
as reassurance. I think of a shirt
I spotted with red wine, and the camellia's tuck
frilling gloss leaves, and of my way
of visualising wounds to match my hurt.

Thundery Saturdays

Sonic dissonance. Somewhere there's a bull
head-butting a microphone in the clouds,

wiring about to blow a fuse.
You're cooking frogskinned omelettes, a red swirl
igniting to a spattered hiss,
a jumpy meteor in the pan
assimilating chopped mushrooms,
a Martian texture mapped into the fold,

domestic interludes, pressure outside,
a mauve sky pushing to come in,
a glass handle on the single raindrop
slinkily flashes at the window,

imitating a transparent fullstop.
Herbs are a later addition. I look
over your shoulder at a brightening sun
lifting around a metal rim.

Thunder's delayed. No breakage in packed clouds,
no abrupt frisson, tonic shower.
Your hair freaks loose, a second omelette glowers

the colour of nasturtiums, and the bull
turns heel after a last brainstorming roar.

Hawthorn

Scent in their flowering's massive like a storm
oppressively laid-back, red conical

surfeit of pungent blossom like a sweet
prepared for Ludwig, a pink mass
of sugared candies buttoned on to paste,

armagnac lacquering the artefact
spooned at with no interest to eat.

Hawthorn was Proust's trigger to get
childhood backtracked into an endless loop

repeating on the page.
He took them to metaphor like brides

in the sensual evening rain.
The berries are tincture for the heart,
homeopathic alchemy,

pimply presented to the thrush.
Heady ferment in the May air
they're yeasty, and turn back on being sweet

to keep one quizzing for a clue
to how they got that way. They're little Alps

when white, conjunctival eyes,
nothing to look at when the flowers go.

I savour their epiphanic credo,
their nowness, colliding with my drive
to push a poem up on a tall lead

and tag it like a kite in windy skies.

November Moonlight

Arrives like a precisional pin-light
isolating a singer's face. Dead-on.
Impacted mountains, planetary flaws
loaded on to my retina
as something like a dilated headlight
dipping through cloud. I upend perspective

to visualize its mass. One million
Earths telescope into the moon,
the long drop had a stoned Li Po
dive for the thing as death-consummation
a way of dying into light,
crazy implosion without oxygen,
the upside-down moon the size of his head.

I work in a dark room to have its blaze
touch at my edges like a sketch
of who I'll be without anatomy –
a buzzy neurosurgeon's diagram,

postbiological halo.
Affluent white light skids across the trees
from a dead source, stellar mausoleum,
stunningly suggestive this autumn night
printed out in severe contrasts
like a nocturnal Brassai, black and white.

Patron Saint Of Eyeliner

Thistles

Almost to shoulder-height. Flat purple heads,
tufty mohicans, blunt imperatives

delivered by their off-limits profile.
The bee executes a centre parting

in going in. They have the tortured line
of Giacometti's anorexics

spines bitten with such spiky pins.
Nobody dares a bare hand to their blaze,

their yogi-postured verticality.
Once, on white, sharded, incandescent sand,

my naked foot tucked glass into a fold.
I learnt the shock of angular surprise;

the blood was a coin-sized red octopus
waving its tentacles across warped skin.

I'm careful up-close to this mobbish bump
of S & M dressed flowers. Glitter-down

in distribution looks like a soft bird
was plucked collectively. All feathers out.

A ritual sacrifice. They'll go like clouds
in autumn, halos teething on the air.

Star-Jasmine

Olfactory cocktail. Swarming nebulae
of bushy perfume, I'm blown back
light-headed with invasive shock
at white attack

this seething coming-clear moment
with white up front, white noise, and seen
earlier a white incident,
a girl linked to a man without a face
confetti spotting in her hair
outside the Chelsea Town Hall, his features
erased by a camera's explosive flash,

the whole group like a cyber artefact.
White is an Agnes Martin white on white
it's the re-entry corridor
to consciousness after some time away.
It's doing writing on the air.
It's hallucinating the dusty sun
as a white billiard ball.

Star-jasmine inside my flat
getting the upper hand as the one scent.
I read beside it. My white walls
are white for thinking on, my mind runs up
their blank presenting faces like a cat.

Brooches

Diamanté ice-spray on her coat,
a fixed dazzle, tear-shaped eye
that's liquid on a black lapel,

or some days it's a soapy moonstone hints
at planets in her blood, or twisted out
along a spiral galaxy's
windstorms, pulsars, explosive nebulae,
a constellation raygunned through,
bright constant among fire-tailed variants.

I look for her accessory splashes,
a seahorse on a jumper, a badged pin,
the pieces picked from market-stalls,
acquisitive jabs at detail

affording her identity.
I like to think a jackdaw came with one,
a sparkly cluster in its beak,
urgent from theft, dropped it through the window

and excitedly flew away.
A Saturday, she'll comb tables,
come home with a new radial, show me how

positioning has stars burn in the spray.

The Word

I want it like a berry on my tongue,
experiential flavour, sharp and sweet
like prickly summer raspberries,

and vocalized with musicality
the word will tango on the page
storm with impulsive encounter
from the ebony Beckstein top
to virtuoso spotlighting,

ocelot-spotted metaphor.
Men wait in deserts, sit on a car roof
anxious for discourse from a star,
or find the thing through pedic sex

inside a Perugia shoe.
I listen for a tremolo, a cue
to dance with language, cut the string
on which the dress depends
for its black smoochy skin.

The word may be an irritant,
a twitch along the spine, a rose
puckering from asymmetrical lips,

a throaty, hedonistic flower.
Sometimes I'm smoky with its tones
of slow cajolement or burnt through

by red alert.
I lyricize its vibrancy,
this nomadic lover returned again
to have me sing of pleasure, sing of hurt.

SET THEM UP JOE

Poe's Marriage Night

Praying for Sister Morphine in the dark
and all poppy derivatives, he trained
spiral coitus with a corkscrew's tip

into a rose-blushed cork,
and had his young bride sleep inside a shroud
and not a clingfilm negligee,

tubercular blood on the sheet
instead of a virgin's rich currency
the colour of sweet williams.

His necrophilic subtext ruled the night,
he who could only love her dead,
preserved her like a florist's rose,

her thirteen years so fragile in his arms,
he saw her dreams transparently
quiver like fish in sinewy current.

But later, rising to the thunder rain,
he went downstairs, and pacted with his need,
and crippled oaks were crying out

and in his vision she was blue
from rigor mortis, but without decay,
and he was with her in her vault,

tormented, mad, priapic, brainstormed-lust
roaring inside his arteries,
her toes splayed out before they turned to dust.

Another Story Of O

September in the park. She sits and waits,
geraniums bleed around a stone lion,
a dark green Citroen's parked by the gates.

So much has happened. She has aged ten years
into a perverse, unrequited love,
and when she looks to establish arrears

of discipline, it's a stranger's gloved hand
can't ever duplicate those cryptic marks
rubbed out like children's diagrams in sand.

She musses expensive highlighted hair,
takes taxis to the chateau, sits outside;
his car has rusted. Fog haloes the air.

She wonders if he's gone to the world's end,
a pink island, and entertains a girl
in supple ways she should or shouldn't bend

to know his mastery. She bites her lip,
the coffee interacts with consciousness,
and recollects how he would have her strip

in public places. And he will come back,
he'll burn her novel, drive to Antibes,
and if his hair is white, his skin-tone slack,

she'll love him all the more. She looks again,
a car door clicks, a man is standing there,
eyes centred on her, and it starts to rain.

Trakl

Wedging red berries in his mouth,
or out flat, head tilted towards a peak

shelved in the moody autumn sky,
he'd line cocaine and expand with the rush
like someone swimming in the lake
whose arms appear to catch the sun

in its 5 p.m. fireballed glow.
October 1912. It's all he knows
in real time, and his sister's near,

frisking her skirt up to her hips
to let him see. He's spectatorial.

Two deer break cover. Fluent gold.
A jackdaw pinks an acorn to trapeze

in tiny ricochets. His mind is blown,
he doesn't ever want captivity,
work as a knife pinned through his palm,

enrolment on the microfiche.
The lake is choked with clouds. Moody cerise.

He turns over. The last sun on his back.
His sister simulates placing a gun
inside her throat. They're desperate

to outlive life. Overhead, the first star
twinkles a footlight on the furzy track.

Spook

Chord-changes trafficked in the spine.
I think it's middle vertebrae the riff
alerts me, like someone had placed
a hand there in the crowd, just laid it flat
and in the doing walked away.
The fingerprints remain like a tattoo.

Something from childhood doubled, paralleled
my absent frequencies. A sack
developed arms and ran across a field.
I waited for the surf to deliver a king
on empty beaches. Empty light

reverberating with aircraft
an engine nacelle flashing out of cloud.
Sometimes I wake up thinking a whole green apple
is sitting on my tongue. I've lost the words

to give experience
authority. A glitch in my system.
And still it's there behind the wardrobe door,
a genderless volume, a split shadow
psyching my pre-sleep vulnerability
as though I expected a black bear-shaped
disarming revenant with masking-tape

to cut club-feet across the floor.

Remains

Deposited in a strong-box at sea
my periwinkle coloured eyes,
my nut-shaped heart,

my bones and cartilaginous residue
to go to fire. Pepper-pot sprinkled ash

from the heat-flash.
My inspiration corked in a bottle,

the gold-eyed genie in vintage
kicking like summer lightning in the dark.

All of me somewhere when I'm gone
to be a light in a dead sun,

my eyelashes particularly
dyed aquamarine for a stage pin-up,

my lips kept on someone's mirror
to receive red pouty kisses,
my poems left to fill a pyramid

for browsers in the Sahara
chased back to grizzled Range Rovers

by a cobalt-footed Egyptian god.

House Of Pain

The room number's written up in fresh blood,
a desperate calligraphy.
I threw the rusty key into a lake

to be gut-swallowed by a pike.
I play my Leonard Cohen songs all night
as empathetic counterpoint
to how a death-train pulls along my veins,

compartments stacked with sleek coffins.
If there are others here, they fax their lives
as information, and avoid

the treachery of corridors. My room
smells of sheened ivy, or car upholstery,
brown leather tanning in the sun.
I load my metaphors into a gun.

The place is off-limits. I bleach in light.
If I get out, you'll never recognize
the person I've become in my black clothes,
listening for rain, as someone waits for love

there in the middle of the deep blue night.

Bacon's Ultimate Heroes – The Hayward Gallery

For John Balance and Peter Christopherson

The river's pushing weights in tedium,
its khaki-cloured, muscled undertow
spined with disjecta, logoed with the cans
badging a loopy current's choppy flow
downrivered under Waterloo
as rain blinds in, a brilliant April shower.
Inside, hulked musculature's on display,
a bodybuilder's flayed anatomy
can't lift itself from the disaster site
to start again, autopsied bulk
delivered like the river's food
in cold blood to a shattered beach.
We stay the physical assault,
dodging the up-front unconfrontable,
and window pinks and greens, a self portrait
in which the artist nightworlds, black on black
bunched in his shadow like a crow.
We ledge outside the café, zoom to chance
a view over the river, and the clouds
are stucco-coloured on the move,
like they're another city in the sky,
and one that's always crashing. We arrest
the moment in our talk, and throw our eyes
to gappy, asymmetrical landmarks,
space-hop to Soho, then to Lloyds,
and take the stormy South Bank on our skin
as though it alerted a neural map.
We speak of Bacon and rough trade,
his self-revulsion, and a last time read
the concrete alphabet, the tumbling clouds,
part on the bridge, and go our separate ways
across the river, as the rain slams in,
its colours flowering in the streaming tide.

Jeremy Reed

Money

I left a broken key inside the lock,
a warped impediment. Bad luck.
A twist obstructing fluency.

The night god's a hole in the wall
dispenser, bright green numerals
displaying how an energy's
solvent or blocked. I punch requests
like an autopsy on my life

and wonder how a man can be these facts
and not his poetry.
The lyric in me colours gold

with the hot bite of imagery.
I see instead of a display
a window into deep black space
where angels swim on frequencies
connected to my fingertips.
The stars are my true currency.

My card's returned without money,
a slick rejection in the night
like being turned down by a date.
I go back home and magic words

to compensate, and think one day
I'll need no money on the last journey
the going home to meet a different light

that's burning always somewhere in the heart.

Empty Pockets

Pike alligatoring a lily pond,
policing all minor fish, best rise to bait
post-sundown, played out of the murk,

nocturnal agents, undercover kings
spotted like termited oak leaves.
I drag my pockets, searching for
a serendipitous windfall?
Check dead statements gone red, blood-red,

I'm like a body cleaned of its insides
by taxidermy. Now I'm bled

I should be lighter for the air,
the poems circulating in my head,
my constituting nobody.

I'm disconnected from the source
of constellating energy.
My gold is minted into lines
that stay unwatermarked, lines got like pike

from the explosive dark. Pure gold
is a crowned lion sleeping in the sun.
An auric halo round inspiration.

This Lloyds, this Nat West, summit on hard cash,
imposing names cut into consciousness.
I try for a time, go pike fishing
in ponds roofed over by black lily pads

still searching in my way for the real thing.

Off License

I slide there, red leaves sucking underfoot,
sopping October mosaic
heeling me damson, orange toes.
I'm walking tree-stuff down the gradient,
the pavement's glossy membrane, up again.

Most nights, I make that journey in the dark.
Compulsive habit, an unconscious need
for union with the bottle; and the shop
has a lighthouse's sanctuary,
a white eye in this London street,
a terminal too brightly lit,

but personable, the two inside
stepping out of a Paul Bowles short story,
diffident, detached, courteous.
I go for Bordeaux reds, a St Emilion,
a Bourgone Pinot Noir, wines which are black,
attentive in their palate notes,
deep with a textured flintiness,
Southern light poured into a glass.

My regularity; I question it
along the route, the place I'm going to,
the extra weight I carry back,
the drinking of that gain.

By day, my night-point is demystified.
Avoid that place, I tell myself,
the quirky metabolic lows at noon,
the dehydrated downs, the off the map
disappearance holes, wait until the work

is burning edges, and the clouds
are shot through by a white diffusive moon.

On The Outside

He tells me bits of woody narrative,
a legendized apostasy
which breaks like winter cherry into flower,

transparent, celebratory spray.
His father was a gangster, all chalk-stripes,
intransigent dictates, an underground
leather-chaired oracular king
self-styled in a green Aston Martin,

East in the pre-development.
He hunts his narrative from cell clusters,
the man he left, cracking the ring
into component halves, quotation marks
placed on a shared pillow.

Back of the story there's a wife
sorting through fragments, bleeding out
betrayal, and it never stops
voice-overs of a broken heart.

We sit across a table, snow outside,
the parked car's a white elephant.
There's a myth in the first pink camellia's wound

turning externals to the air
in all its full, stagy impromptu part.

Set Them Up Joe

Whisky turns memory to blurred amber,
woody associations, rolling fire.
The big smack to the nerves, the bar mirror

glinting with auroral icebergs
seen from a ship lifting with swell,

somebody waving a red shirt
from a cruising toppler.

In Soho whisky bites like a tiger,
coloured like bronze chrysanthemums,
untamed by water.
Hart Crane smashed chair-legs drinking Cutty Sark,

cirrhotic bravado.
A malt distinction; it tastes of those days
we know we're older, but we're young,

and turn to the red creeper on the wall
as Octoberish consolation.

Their trade names are like sound-poems,
clan histories. This man's so shot with it,
he legendizes days, trips on his tongue,

retrieves the lost blue of his eyes
into a centred focus for a hit.

John Keats And Pippins

I'm skinning oranges to scent a fire
with tartish peel. John Keats is flying kites
or writing odes in a dark bar
three streets away. His lungs are two red fish.
His dragonish kite's concertinaed shut,

the waitress couldn't care less for the vine
snaking its loaded black fruit through his hair.
Berries splash on the page; the waiting car
is polished, closed and sinister.
He checks it through the window. It will wait,
complete with a white-gloved chauffeur.
The waitress dreams she will become a star,

John Keats imagines bees swarming
out of his girlfriend's blueish eyes.
Blood on his handkerchief. The chromed limo
has come from Highgate cemetery,
sedate precision on a leaf-blotched road.

I'm glossing pippins in my flat,
a robin's belly glows on each apple.
John Keats closes his notebook, goes on out,
the waitress punching eye-holes in his back
and stormed by blasting scarlet leaves
ducks in the car and knows what it's about.

Brit Poetry

A two-dimensional hang-up.
There's no quark
or quantum leap into the visionary,

representational surfaces are flat.
Nobody ODs on a burn-out speed
towards a whizzing parallax,
an overflight, ufonauts in a ship,

the poet as receptive contactee.
Nobody's taking risks. The footage reads
as face-up nose-square documentary;

the damage limitation to the nerves observed.
From Primrose Hill to St John's Wood
Blake visualized a city roofed with gold,
each body cell an interface

connected to a corresponding star.
An inspirational neural galaxy.
Why are the weird and wired the absentees

on the Brit poet's mobile? Grey not pink.
The whole social thing crowds like blue algae
polluting clear waters, toxicity
coating the king-salmon's flash-trust.

Nobody's action-painting on the page
or hanging in with the millenium
or looking for the messenger

to stop the car, point it off the high road,
insert the implant, dematerialize,
and be as quickly headed for a star.

Verlaine

He's the bad onion who we rarely peel,
the fade-out part in every narrative,

the one who watched genius implode,
a spotty schoolboy catch a star
like it was a gold spider in his hand
trapezing visionary calligraphy

across a flagging ear of corn.
Verlaine's the witness not the counterpoint
to genius; all DT's, hysterical

possessiveness, rarely able to choose
between a woman and a man.
A beetling satyr; volcanic testosterone.

Absinthe was white light to his brain,
hallucinating doubles, so impaired,
he'd fight his image in the bar mirror,
run blank against the impostor,

wormwood revenge. Ferretish eyes,
a way with musicality,
transparent lyric blue like air,
like Rimbaud's eyes.

A vagrant mostly, in his dusted coat,
le poete maudit, a cause celebre
for dissolution, shuffling through the streets

towards an angel with flying red hair.

A DANGEROUS GAME

Vampire

Back of the shop I found this shoe,
a sachet wedged in the stiletto point,
blood category, path-lab details scored out,

a stormy blonde on haberdashery,
checking her nails, I didn't see her look
right through somebody, two neat holes
got there as laser precision,
I only saw the person flashed

by devastating hallucination.
Odd in the lift, a rusty horseshoe hung
on a protrusive black-eyed nail,

a zigzag tear in the mirror.
A Jean Harlow pretender, I was stuck
with the blonde coming back at me,
perfect proportions, scarlet mouth

owning to a congealed blood-drop,
a little something like a crushed berry.
I remembered old woods I'd known, a girl
whooshing from trees in a white sheet
with cut-out slits for nose and eyes,

and later someone snitched by fangs.
I went back to the street, my jugular
alive with nerves, a stray presentiment
warning me I was followed, targeted,

and under pressure, under heat.

Jeremy Reed   121

A Dangerous Game

Incurably distraught, I wait them out
in Mayfair, Green Park, the King's Road,
or question Soho for a certain face
to overdramatize the biting hurt
of keeping yours up-front in memory,

a red-haired interface in ruined nerves,
obstructive presence that I can't get round
for need that has me open-armed
and walking backwards down a moving stair
into the underground. April again,
intoxicating scents cut like a wire,
narcissi, lily-of-the-valley, blue lilacs,

a sharp cocktailed vivacity,
urgently regenerative overload.
Mad love. Fire-tasting L'Amour Fou,
throat full of smoking embers, heart so wired

its fuses might explode.
I look to find the variants of you,
a dangerous game, in every London street,
this one, that one with downturned lips,
overstated makeup, another one
whose comparison is your legs,

but I can't find the half of you
in anyone. I turn my heart over
for what I've lost, had to let go,
relinquished in a mood to hurt myself,
and you are out there, somewhere, making eyes
into a compact, while a grey April
builds avalanching cumuli in high wide skies.

Old Compton Street

Maybe two hundred thousand feet a week
leave no recordable trace on this site,
anonymous as bright, highlighting rain,
they come and go, villaged an hour
in Soho's alleys, searching out
an excitement that always seems contained

like thunder in a lion's mouth,
like the mauve rainbow stepping out of cloud
to dazzle over Meard Court, Boucher Street;
a leather boy caught in parenthesis

between Frith and Old Compton Street
wonders if a sunflower has burst
corolla in a puddle.
A tangy whiff from the Algerian Coffee Store,
cheesy delicatessens, all the rap

at street tables, and overhead gargoyles,
chimeras assembling their own skyline.
They bottle in this artery,
the gay and straight, the polyglot

picking up international magazines.
Black cabs blast through, those amber-eyed
Sisters of Mercy in the night,
raw bustle whirlwinds from the near market.

A street-cred eccentricity
invests the lot. This threshold to the maze
sees two fashion students high-strut

in bodies and clingfilm from St Martin's
to Wardour Street, pink hair like cockatoos,
one holding a red flower in her mitt.

Soho Afternoon

Mauve altostratus soundproofing the sky,
the baroque details up there with the roofs,
griffin and angel staring out of stone,
a drum-machine clicking out perfect beat
from a high window. Who lives there

above the polysemic crowds?
His tattoo shows Kali standing on skulls,
the other arm's a heart with a dagger,
noise simmers like a disturbed hive.

Imagine this village as a desert
just for an afternoon, big shock cacti
exploding into scarlet flower
down Wardour Street, most cars buried in sand,
camels nosing outside the brasserie,
the heat pressurized to a solid flame.

The mirage shifts out of my view.
I get the tension of this place, the feel
of urgent impulse. I will know these streets
only according to my life,

the short or long of it. The taste is now,
the cafés spilling to the street,
the moment huge like sky-high lettering,
3.03 Thursday afternoon
aggrandized in gold-plated reflections
the second after cloud the sun breaks through.

Couple

The lake's like television. Coloured dream.
Cloud traffic wanders over; a red plane
fractals a rapid transition;

a trout flips water for the splashy fly.
She's wall-eyed flat on antipsychotics,
he can't believe she's gone that far
flipping towards an edge, a torched
mansion in which the screen goddess
is brushing fire out of blonde hair,

or so she would identify
in chaos, audiovisual flicker,
her mismatched nouns got from a direct lead

to Marilyn Monroe. Her wired-up head,
his studied calm.
They watch waterbirds contest martial arts

wings beating a staccato slap.
His coat's a loud mix in the lake,
and when she's lucid, energy comes through
like it's all right again, and she points out
the green in a mallard, the blue,

and watches as their webbed feet bike across
a surface organized into love-hearts.

Death Party

A taxi loiters somewhere in the wood,
diesel reverberations, a slammed door's
percussive statement, crisp steps rapping out
precise direction under oaks,
a jay's declamatory hysteria

gunned from high branches. Slow September light
making the clearing where they're grouped,
ten of them, all dressed formally,
white shirts, dark suits, and one detached,
standing back up against a tree,
he wears black shades, has stepped into himself

and seems the regulating power
which activates the scene. Conflicting oaks
drag at a heady breeze. The arrival
carries a chunky red valise,
his ways are tentative, even his smile

travels from corners and retracts.
Eleven? And they await another one.
They pour wine into paper cups, and keep
alert vigil under the trees,
a gang from houses along Shadwell Stair?

Another taxi? The engine killed dead.
They're waiting for him in his black Teddy Boy's coat
and string tie to articulate
a way of sacrifice, a shot ring out
sending jays spilling up into the air.

Anamnesis

A rusty biscuit tin buried in sand;
he couldn't relocate the spot.
Lovers had lain there, breath like raspberries,

saliva index bonding, pairing out
two destinies. August in thistley fog.

His time spent in retrieval. Blueprinted,
he'd dropped through a re-entry corridor,

remembered everything, dipped in a lake
and watched the colours run
to inconsistencies. Brainfade.

A lifetime's disassemblage. Memory
losing its translatable equivalents.
A lighthouse giraffed off that deep blue coast

had been a constant, white giant
waist-deep in water. Bloodshot eye,
typing a language after dark.

Years later, hairy raspberries on a spoon,
he savours captions, lets the rest go blank
like holes puckered in quantum foam,

and watches stars windowed in a night sky,
busy with point-transmissions across space.

First Death

It's like first love, a tooth notched in the heart,
the irreparable tear in seamless youth,
the glitch in the recorded voice,
the act that separates the self
from continuity – I heel in sand
reading a letter on the fly-buzzed beach
at seventeen, a dragging blueblack sea
thunderheads in its undertow, dumping
its download of expiring surf
across slicked pebbles, read a mother's words
about a daughter's, girlfriend's suicide
at Chester Gate, and feel the beach up-end,
my life break like a window at my feet
in jagged impacted shards, the disbelief
thrown like a planet at the sun,
an up in arms rejection of the fact
of Paula's OD in her little room
bursting on Regent's Park. The wave
returned, indifferent phosphor beating out
the universal rhythm, orange peel
and cans junked in the squashy froth.
I came back every day as though
the place was shock absorbent of her death,
obsessively returned to this one beach
through autumn, winter, wide-set, seething tides
smashing discursive dialogue
around the headland, tried to place her now
in mental space, hold on to something known
against her being sucked through a black hole,
reconstituted what I knew, and came
to live with that, and fast-tracked through the years
retained her blue eyes in my own,
and something like a love affair with death,
first death, and how it signalled through hot tears.

Love And Hate

Fuming November and the pre-dark roar
of Piccadilly, we despite the crowds
framed in the instantaneity of love,
salival genies dancing where our tongues
met as a glitter-ogive, I could taste
the sweet and hurt in you, the undertow

of who you are, as though a flashback screened
you in a childhood moment, quite alone,
learning that death existed for yourself
as well as others like a stone
reddens inside a ripening peach.
You as a punkish rebel in the park
discovered by my taste-buds, you again
printing your volatility
in hot-spots in my busy mouth.

Everything meeting at its breaking point
inside the heart; we backed against a shop
hearing explosions in the sun
knowing the future open like a door
giving direct on to a stormy sea,
a lick of dazzle smoking on the shore,
a blinding wall of blue infinity.

Pacted by love and hate we swore to learn
by separation, keep apart
to know a truth, how love deepens by pain
into a common angel, and your hair
was violent sunset-red, you turned to go,
my life vibrating in your blood
as little earthquakes, I who'd face you round
reclaim your hand and mount the highest stair.

Loss

Deeply at three to four each afternoon,
displacement, loss of gravity, I try
for reclamation in my heart,

extract you to be ravaged by my thoughts
the way I watch red bird-cherries
ripped at this instant by a jay
loading its craw, immediate

shrieking avian vitality.
And loss is weight, intangibly
supported through the years, today an hour
feels like driving into the blank
of foreign towns – I've forgotten the name

and only small details remain,
the couple joined as a red oval mouth,
mobbingly loud geraniums,
the undertaker's black polaroid front,
a highrise like a vertical aquarium.

But loss, the human in me missing you,
means dropping through an air pocket,
my feet making no contact with the ground.
I go outside to cherry stones
pinked under trees, and listen to my heart
beating out absence, trying to get free
of old containments, and the jay breaks off,
triggers up shrieking to another tree.

Chrysanthemums

They smell of train journeys in late summer,
Jacques Brel's "J'arrive" – the yellow ones
crowdy, the size of a grapefruit,
or as a second preference russet
like autumn in its mellowing
amber sunlight behind it, smoky mist
remaining as a halo.

September's like a hazel eye
dreaming in a scummed over pond
a twist of iodine parachuting
through clear water. Chrysanthemums
are inscrutably compact,
butch hairdos layered to a jagged beehive,
they end up ceremonially
in cemeteries. Flowers for the dead.

I like their volume. Two or three
keeping domestic vigil in a flat
like freeze-framed samurai. I'll take the train
with autumn tap-dancing in scarlet shoes
on every station, passing through
to meet a platform where somebody waits
with flowers in the foggy rain –

a livid yellow torch as a salute.

Amaryllis

Constricted throats, won't let the secret out
at first appraisal, a first date
on heady, anticipative purchase,

and carried upright like a torch,
give reddish hints of their dramatic flare,
their sometime orgiastic abandon
days later with the diva thing,
onomatopoeic register,

they're Callas singing a posthumous aria,
hedonistic orality,
vocal exercises that last all day,
lividly sexual in my flat,

exact in disciplined control.
They're cold, despite their propositioning,
their invitation to fellatio,
their open vowel note-endings spelling out

scandalous discourse. Red. Red. Red.
They invite Latin associations,
a girl one summer on the whitest beach
owning to a flower name, and that she sings,

gone home the next day, but she leaves with you
a Tuscany address, a black-eyed look
to nurture in October rains, a smile
you get back buying shocking flowers
to place a sultry temper in a living space.

Running Out Of Time

It spears up neck-high into swirlish runs,
chaotic purple loosestrife. That's its thing,
raffish regeneration, poking out
for violent rains. Really we came this way
talking of flash incisive speed
in poetry, Tom Raworth's poetry,
and how perception jumps from a motel
on the edge of a mauve desert,
the poster showing as a blaze

cholla cacti in the Santa Catalinas
to this ropy aqueduct where we lean
above an oval pond wedged thick
with waterlily pads. A middish afternoon
late August, and include in it
a Paul Smith label on a cotton shirt
and bits of identity ephemera
carried as evidence that here means now
in all our overstrained impermanence,

and speed not usually wired into poetry
exists in this copy of Big Green Day,

and shouldn't we state it's obligatory
poets mind-bend to altered consciousness,
and purple loosestrife, we walk through the lot
jungled by cold flame swimming at our necks.

THREE SONGS
FOR MARC ALMOND

Blood Roses

Lyrics for Marc Almond

Since you went over
    to another lover
I lie on an ostrich-plumed bed,
    Caligula, Nero,
Oscar Wilde as a hero
    of liberative sex
is how we advance.
But I'm here with my tableau
of lost loves, my trousseau,
    and I float in a vortex
where drowned sailors dance.
And I'd shoot myself in the head.
    Jean Genet, Garcia Lorca,
    I offer you blood roses,
Arthur Rimbaud, Paul Verlaine,
I feel more than certain
    your lives knew a moment
    outside such long torment,
when the fire in your wine glass
    was the red of the sunset;
but since you went over
    to another lover
my heart's on a blade of regret.
    I visit your gravestones
in the rain and I'm alone.
And I'd shoot myself through the head,
but I'm waiting for your dead hands
    to hold mine in the sunshine,
    waiting for a bracelet
    inscribed by Caligula,
    Nero, Garcia Lorca,
and for the red rose to open
    in my own glass of wine.

Smoking Ruins

Lyrics For Marc Almond

Love in a graveyard, in smoking ruins,
it seems very hard
to be one of a number
who gather in alleys, a backyard,
or a palace
built of dreams and black lace.
I remember your face
in those ruins and the ash
that dusted your feet.
Love in a graveyard, in smoking ruins,
the redhead of carnations,
the exchanged assignations
in the ruins before dawn.

There's always the lost ones
who place orange roses
for the anonymous in ruins,
and in springtime mimosas
for those without names.
Love in a graveyard, in smoking ruins,
has it ever been this hard
to claim an identity,
love in the ruins for those who aren't free.

Funeral Mirror

Lyrics for Marc Almond

Youth's an illusion
an extended delusion
we've outgrown before twenty,
my address book is empty
    of those assignations
that once gave me pleasure.
You can look for the treasure,
a blue stone in my heart's
    blue and black ashes,
pink cummerbunds, sashes,
for I promised to wear it
as a ring at your funeral,
    in the slow black car,
when you're buried by one star,
    and the light of a candle,
by Hermione, Querelle,
    your fictitious lovers,
and your obstinate monsters.

And there'll be time to reflect
when we drive back through the night,
    back through the Black Forest
lit up by processions,
    of the ghosts of your lovers
    who've all broken cover
in earrings and jewelled shrouds,
of how we looked in the mirror
    on the day of your death,
    and wrote in red lipstick
your name and your age
and your love of the stage,
    as we hold up a cobra
    on a black burning stick.

Jeremy Reed   139

POSTHUMAN BLUES

Concentrated Orange Juice

Lifting a Californian sun
inside my glass, stringy vivacity
lining the lip, it's a pulpy red core

surfs on the mouth's convexity,
demands I'm everything inside that taste,
that fridge-cooled wacky meteor
immunising my chemistry,
boosting my antibodies, a tiger

flushing my cells, a concentrate
giving me speed. Girls with red hair
are shocking if they're Japanese,
hair the colour of Jaffa oranges

doused in vermilion. Red Masako,
an orange Hariko.
Three black clouds shaping a haiku

in direct line of the sunset.
I go for livid fibre on this winter's day,
a jump-start to my energies,
and the idea of oranges as art,
a column built beside a second one,

fruit-padded muscles of the orange god
supported by black fishnet tights.
Dramatic tiger-lilies in the room;

outside, the day is finding pace,
its many orange possibilities begun.

2 Billion Tomorrows

Summer was maddening red geraniums,
the days tucked under leaves, aircraft traffic
piling up metal in the sky.

Ear to the ground, a seismic database
was audibly pitched from the underworld.
The cracks showed later, like a biker used
a silo for speed rehearsals,
impacted tyre-treads cut into the floor.

I loved you all along nervous highways.
July to August. In Some Like It Hot'
the sequins dance along Marilyn's line
optimally eroticized.
We watched the film in twitchy heat; your dress

was lightning down the spinal zip.
The air was currant mixed with amino acids,
the prospect of 2 billion tomorrows

impossible for other lovers, other days,
we living in the moment, using up
our quota, biting lip to lip.

Reactivator

A friend this autumn afternoon
consoling, up above the street,
a few spiky anemones,
Maison Bertaux, and the wall opposite,
Wilde's Kettners, the light solitary
from our big galaxy, it's red honey
translated into metaphor.
I tell myself there are no physical bodies
free-floating through inner space, collisions
don't happen inside.

You are there,
but where are we situated? The beat
is molecular energy
toned to a rhythm by the heart. I see
a pink tiered pastry demolished
in fragmentary stages. We're of this time,
like it or not, it's easier to think
backwards or forwards, the immediate

is where we are, I need your hand
an hour or two, this redgold day,
Soho pulsing as a backdrop
in a diagrammatic diaphragm,
a new youth deciding what's in, what's out,
the tension now as no other –

I whisper, but I want to shout.

Heartbreak Hotel

The blue Cadillac parked outside the place
was really his. The car's a memento
of rock aggrandisement. I've known that street,
reached it at the dead end of night
with no hope in my fingers or my mind,
and love a scorched heart smoking in the rain
to be the subject of a rock lyric,
a drinking straw stuck into a rich vein.

Get into the hotel, there's no-one there.
Of course, his song is playing all night long,
and outside must be Lonely Street,
a sort of desultory mausoleum
where all the broken hearted lovers wait
for some redemption: summer gold,
or a felicitous stranger who's been
about to show for years. The bluest night.
I placed my hands on the warm Cadillac,
as though it had been driven across State
for 20 hours, it was that hot,
and rain was steaming off the bodywork.

Chapter 8

Posthuman evolution in the lab,
he used to spend his days mutating genes,
then lunchbreaks feed a Porsche his snappy foot,
tread the accelerator flat, and burn
distinctions of a conifered landscape
to an imploded blue forested rush,
a wacky blur full of the loud music
co-opted into his mad dash
to meet her in the clearing. Mushroomed clouds
were part of this, topheavy cumulus
standing like blocks of time above a lake's
obsidian surface. She would wait for him
on the rear-seat of her customised Saab,
silk stockinged legs draped over a headrest,
a life-sized Barbie doll sat at the wheel
to simulate appearances.
His mind would be bleeping with formulae,
gene management, prosthetic utopias,
and he would bring to her positioning,
the complex geometries of sex
she'd never visited, her vaulted lips
enunciating new vocabularies
of pleasure finding woody notes in pain.
Their ritual meeting happened twice a week
by a disused log cabin, jays screaming
in forest scaffolding. Today he brought
configurations he called Chapter 8
to her variant elasticity,
and she would next time add a Chapter 9
and speak it out loud as he placed her right,
toes wriggling the way small fish smooch a pond
before the thunder, and the rain's fast shine.

Hell

A hexed computer screen. The microwave
pixillated with black angels,
and in the underground car park, concrete
is broken up obstrusively,
a chapel with red drapes is underneath.

A death-warp comes to cities in the afternoon,
a no-time zone, zero metabolism,
the earth stops rotating for half an hour,

a blackout, blank in consciousness,
only the weird ones in operation,
the shadow running without a shadow,

the UFO prowling above the desert.
Inside the chapel, a dominatrix
watches a poppy grow out of a book.

I stand against a solid wall
in Doc Martens. A hearse hums down the street.
Aliens jump out the car. One fires a gun

right through a close-up blackly spinning sun.

Jumping The Centuries

He checks his entry point. The mirror shows
somebody walked out of the 18th century
into our own. He calls himself De Sade.
He's slightly fazed or jet-lagged, marginally
dissociated. It's all missing time
those years spent as a set of impulses
in or around his chateau. Purple vines
gone rusty by November, a black car
depositing inquisitive tourists,
long days that had some meaning in his growth,
two lovers staring madly from the heights.
Now he sits concealed in a black limo
negotiating city streets. The rain
is constant, and it's all like film.
The limo stops outside a mansion block,
and this time he's affirmative he's gay,
the young man inside making up for him,
answers the buzzer, shows the stranger where
he can take off his clothes, extract his nerves,
and jump three centuries in a single day.

Roderick Usher Resurrected

What if he swam clear like a water rat
after the turbulence, his sleek body
oiled by the violent moonlight, and the house

was still there in its ivied straitjacket,
his sister, naked in the music-room,
playing the piano with her stockinged feet,
the mobile lacquered with the red
polish she used on livid fingernails

presented as sheathed artefacts?
What if his persecution mania
was in remission, and he touched the walls
to empathize with their stability,
and snaked his tongue along his sister's spine

to a cautionary off-limits tattoo.
What if he sat in his red leather chair,
no longer obsessed by a netted eye
twitching in a taut spider's web,
no longer hearing white noise circulate
around the house, melismatic whistles,

his sister's vocalized distress in sleep?
What if he exchanged his suit for her dress,
left his sopping pelt on the floor,
went out like that into the deeper night,

flagged down a car, and looked round a last time
to see his wild-haired sister running in pursuit?

Invisible Writing

No-one will tell you it's de-globalized,
the word with all its tangy lemon scent
and sparkling upfront metaphor,
in from the Gobi desert, or somewhere
eagles inhabit, out of bounds,

ball-lightning saucering through racy air.
Most of your life you've gone its way –
poetry written on the wall
bigger than ideologies
living without captivity
like lions somewhere ruling a grass plain.

No-one will tell you it's contexualized,
the word is looped to samples, looped again
into an ambient surf, anonymous
event in which we all participate.
The chill out room's a place to meditate,
an ice palace. If we should get away
it's to a virtual capital,
a champagne glass left on the beach
the magnum bigger than a fort.

No-one will supplement his work with blood;
the thought-police want it clean. No-one will write
a terra firma elegy
by the Black Sea.
The poem reddening on a flinty vine.

Once there was DNA inside the word,
a double-helixed signature.
Now there is printout and the car at noon
to buy a new designer drug,
the dealer dressed in holographic foil

talking of ways to make the future shine.

Paradise

Somewhere a blowout in the sun.
Mostly the island cities had decayed,
the rich and migrant moved out to the coast,
Naomi Campbell in pink glitter shorts
protected by a UV screen
facing a de-androgynized Bowie

concerned only with the need to survive
beside the Pacific's blue lip, the surf's
unending dialogue with wind, no rain
arriving for years on the beach,
and in the dunes, car-roofs poked through the sand,
a pink stretch limo, the burnished copper
of an actress's vintage Cadillac.
Mostly the airbrushed photographs depict

the one who came down from the hills,
a UFO abductee whose implant fed
his brain with data from a source
located in the stars. Others are there

along the beach, a cellulited Madonna
a born again claiming to be Elvis Presley
in a Las Vegas jacket. Bowie spoons
a green algae jelly pudding

distastefully into his mouth.
Another Californian afternoon,
somebody sniffs oxygen from a can.
The rationed drinks are airline bottles filched

from grounded and decaying jets.
The wind carries printout across the dunes.
Sinatra's voice breezes down the blue air.

Where The Dark Stands Guard

White noise, white heat, the summer lays us out,
I come to meet you and to reconnect
with messages punched through your cells,
the little and big moments on your tongue
like desert flowers cramming their lot
into dramatic intervals of rain.
We meet for fact in Little Newport Street.

And for today I've the apprehension
a sort of minotaur out of its cage
is sniffing round an underground car park,
trailing a red coat in black oil,
trying by phases to arrive at speech.
What if the creature drives across London
in a neurosurgeon's white car

on a kamikaze mission?
You tell me bits about yourself
which stick to me like glass buttons
to be sewn on a cardigan.
A coat of many colours for autumn.

The buildings seem a mirage in the sun,
a warped, hallucinated hologram.
We'd like to plant red poppies by the road,
instruct children in mysteries,
and when I tell you things about myself
you stand back as though each word might explode.

Jeremy Reed   153

Gothic Lit

Heart transplant by a vampire's teeth,
I feel a black wolf from the underworld
snout hackles wet from autumn leaves
against my knee. The ice burials are underway,
the cryogenist slips off gloves, lies back
and feels the helicopter throttle up
above the plant. Two girls have formed a pact
and tube each other. There's a red exhaust
declares itself like dye in fog.
The helicopter chops towards the hills,
they'll note the rock star's long term ice request
and accommodate storage for his glitzy clothes
as well as his preserved body. The night
burns with the last of Hell's Angels
blazing a bike trail for a rendezvous.
Everything's possible, a dripping wolf
zipped into leathers behind the big light,
bound for tomorrow, loaded up on speed,
piling on fuel as though lifting for flight.

Left Overs

Just leaving everything behind. Language
evacuees, words roll across the dust
like bumpy hailstones, expendable things.
Two paramedics sit beside the road,
one has a stuffed owl perched on his shoulder,
the other laces up a purple boot.
They've miscalculated a call,

their van hums with loud input under trees.
Someone may pull the plug by 4 a.m.
the whole galaxy go out light by light.

He's lost in a recording studio,
this one who favours ambient. All the loops
are sampled with industrial sound.
Most people left their cities for the land

and get about.
A biker watches in the hills,
an angel shows sometimes as a fast lick
of radial energy. It's the big day,

the river films the same slow European clouds
as a white tumble on its back.
The circuit fires. And is it go or stay?

ABOUT THE AUTHOR

Jeremy Reed was born in Jersey, Channel Islands. Acknowledged as one of Britain's foremost poets, he has been described by Kathleen Raine as "the most imaginatively gifted poet since Dylan Thomas", and by J.G Ballard as "the most gifted British poet working today".

Between 1984 and 1990 he published six books with Jonathan Cape. Four collections of poetry: By The Fisheries, Nero, Engaging Form and Nineties, and two novels: Blue Rock and Red Eclipse. Penguin published his Selected Poems in 1987, and he has been the recipient of major awards which include an Eric Gregory Award, the Somerset Maugham Award, and the Poetry Society European Translation prize for his version of Eugenio Montale's The Coastguard's House, published by Bloodaxe in 1991.

Among his recent novels are Inhabiting Shadows, Isidore – described by J.G. Ballard as "superb" – and When The Whip Comes Down, all published by Peter Owen. His autobiography Lipstick Sex And Poetry was published to acclaim in 1992, as were his books about the hallucinated imagination, Delirium and Madness, The Price Of Poetry.

His collection of poems Red Haired Android was published by Harper Collins and in the US by City Lights, as was Delirium. Chasing Black Rainbows, a novel about Artaud, and the science fiction novel Diamond Nebula were published in 1994. The same year saw his first publication for Creation Books, Kicks. They have also published his novellas of surreal erotica, The Pleasure Château and Sister Midnight, and his angular trilogy of popular music studies: Marc Almond: The Last Star, Scott Walker: Another Tear Falls, and Brian Jones: The Last Decadent.

Jeremy Reed lives in London, reads extensively on the subject of extra-terrestrials, avoids the literary scene, and is one of the most prolific of contemporary writers.

www.creationbooks.com